The Lord's Revelation

THE ONE WHO WALKS AMIDST THE SEVEN GOLDEN
LAMPSTANDS

GOD'S MESSAGE TO ALL CHRISTIANS WORLDWIDE

2nd Edition

Volume one

For more information about The Lord's Revelation reach us at:

thevictorbooks@gmail.com

Other books by the author:

The One Who Walks Amidst the Seven Golden Lampstands – Volume Two

The Seventh Horn of the Lamb of God's Spoken Mystery of Christ's Body And Blood – The Victors' Weapon In Tribulations

The Appealing Voice of the Sentry Angel "Fear Not I'm With Him"

The Mystery of the Mount of Congregation From the High Priest Melchizedek

The Sixth Horn Of The Lamb Of God And The Warfare Of The Abomination Of Desolation

The Other Comforter

The Living Witness On Earth And In Heaven

The Trilogy of Witnesses: The Comforter, God's Spirit of Grace and Supplication and God's Wisdom

The Ancient of Days and God's Spirit Of Judgement

ISBN 978-1005-7-9243-5

CHAPTER 3
THE ALTAR OF WITNESS

AUTHOR'S NOTE

This is the Second Edition of The Lord's Revelation (THE ONE WHO WALKS AMIDST THE SEVEN GOLDEN LAMPSTANDS) Volume 1. The reason for this second edition is because since the first edition was published in 1986, there is a need for some updates; hence a second edition. Another reason is that the second edition includes two major changes that have greatly improved the first edition, over and above the minor corrections already alluded to. In addition, paragraph numbering has been revised to reflect individual chapters instead of the entire book. Chapter numbering has also been revised, by realigning chapter headings to reflect actual content, thus reducing the total number of chapters.

Another major change in the second edition is the incorporation of the message of The Fifth Horn of the Lamb of God. The Fifth Horn explains and further clarifies certain aspects of Volume One, thus providing a better understanding.

Readers are advised to acknowledge that this book contains a lot of mysteries that require divine enlightenment for true comprehension. For this reason, it should not be read without scriptural accompaniment. In effect the Bible must always be available when reading this book; prayers and fasting should also be utilized.

To reiterate: Do not ever read this book without the Bible. The Bible confirms all aspects of the Revelation, so if you read and you do not understand, take a deep breath, say a prayer, then read it over again and the Lord will provide a more perfect, divine comprehension.

We encourage everyone to endeavour to avail themselves of this new edition which is designed to help them as they strive to find total perfection in the Lord.

May the Lord be with all obedient servants of the Lamb's new Israel. Amen!

PREFACE

"Quench not the spirit, despise not prophesying, but rather prove all things and hold fast to that which is right. Abstain from all forms of evil". 1 Thessalonians 5: 19-22(KJV)

The contents of this book comprise compelling prophetic messages that are devoid of any fault or even a suggestion of doubt. They are prophecies revealed by the Lord God to correct the faith of Christendom by uncovering specific Biblical mysteries and in so doing, allow for a better understanding of the Bible and the truth that is manifest in the spirit of God, which no living being should cast doubt on or question their divinely inspired truth.

Some people believe that prophecies are no longer a divine gift of grace in these end-time days. Others aver that prophecy was a miracle that existed in the past; today it no longer occurs.

The following scriptures, however, emphasize that revelations and prophecies are still very much alive in these end times. If you read: Daniel 12:4-10; 1

Corinthians 14:22 &29; Ephesians 4:10-12;
Revelation 10:11; Proverbs 29:18, these and many
others from the Bible prove beyond doubt that the
miracle of prophecy is not sealed but can be
seamlessly applied to the present day to explain
many mysteries and thus ensure a more perfect
comprehension. These revelations are recorded in
their exact chronological order, to make sure
readers are clear about their source. It is thus left
to all individual readers to decide whether to
embrace or reject them.

Thus sayest the Saviour, the Holy One of Israel: I
the Lord thy God showest thee that which is good
for thee, I guideth thee on the path that thou
taketh. Isaiah. 48:17 (KJV)

HOW IT ALL STARTED

I, Victor Nyarko Amoah and one of our pastors went into the presence of the Lord for three days of fasting and prayer. After substantial supplications before the Lord, we determined to ask for the empowerment of the Holy Spirit; that it would descend into the church as it had been known to do in the olden days. In the early hours of the third day, around 2 a.m. while in fervent prayer beseeching the Lord to improve the spiritual standing of the church and while the pastor was engaged in prayer, at that very moment, the Lord opened my eyes spiritually. My ears were also opened and I heard Him speak.

With divine sight I saw a huge toad, shining like brass, with a shiny inscription on its head that read

"Barr Jessus" which was explained to me as the power of darkness; the enemy of all truth and righteousness. With my understanding of this revelation, I was moved to rebuke it in my prayers and kept saying; "The blood of the Lord rebuke you, evil spirit of toad". This first revelation went away after some time when some liquid was sprinkled on the toad, which after a struggle disappeared.

After a little while, as I was still on my knees praying, I saw a great brightness, stronger than the brightness of the sun. Then I saw a figure in the form of a human being, standing on something in the likeness of clean and gleaming cotton wool.

This sight threw me into awe, and like the first time, I started rebuking it: "May the blood of the Lord rebuke you; you who are revealing yourself to baffle me". But this time, the more I rebuked the vision, the closer it came until it was right next to me. As soon as I opened my mouth to say "The blood of the Lord rebuke you", but instead I spontaneously started describing the exact image of the figure before me and all my prayers subsequently became the narration of my vision. As I contemplated the image, I saw that his head and hair were pure white, like snow. Some pillars surrounded the image in the form of lampstands. They were all of equal height and about the same height of the image of the man standing amidst them; they were also shining very brightly.

The man was dressed in an attractive linen robe with a military officers' belt strapped across his shoulder and on his chest. Several ornamental decorations emblazoned the belt in a shining array. The man's eyes were like burning candles and his legs were like a mass of brass brightened in a hot furnace. He fixed his gaze on me and when our eyes met, I covered my face immediately because the brightness emanating from his face was too strong, like the reflection of bright sunshine on a mirror; unbearable to the eyes. The sight of this man really frightened me, and I was weakened.

Then the man took my right hand and drawing me closer to him, he placed his hand on my palm and said: "Look, son of man, fear not, open your eyes, arise, straighten your face and listen to these messages". His voice sounded like thunder resonating from afar. He told me: "Son of man, on the day you prayed and asked for power from Heaven to proclaim the gospel from your church and spread it among the nations, I chose at the very same time to abide with you and confirm your testimony with my power. But you, after you made your prayers, failed to fulfill your vow and are therefore not found righteous in this instance, for having deceived me, the root of David, the Alpha and Omega. He went on to say; "Son of man, compare your actions to an invitation to the state authority of your nation that honours your invitation and arrives with a mighty army and other retinues, only to meet your absence; you failed to attend the meeting to which you had invited him. Would your ruler still consider you to be righteous? Likewise, would you ever find favour before God if you take a vow and then forsake it?"

Now, you Victor, son of man, the reason you are able to see me face to face is because of your prayers, especially your request to be shown the way in which to lead the church. As a reply to your request, "I arose to save those who are worthy of salvation". You asked for wisdom, realization and understanding to enable you to lead the flock home in safety, so have I revealed myself to you for your steadfastness. Know that no human being can lead another human being to eternal life if I do not show him the way. There are many in church leadership and the priesthood, who have never asked for wisdom from Me and they fool themselves into complacency and self-exaltation.

Look, Moses never knew the way from Egypt to Cannan but he applied faith and requested of Me to be shown the right path and he was given counsel from God so he would not lead the Lord's nation astray. Thus I, in disguise, led the nation of Israel out of the wilderness at the hand of Moses.

There are many who are in church leadership and the priesthood today, who do not know that they must humble themselves and ask and receive from Me the wisdom needed to empower them to carry out their duties. Look! There is none, who abide in the weakness of the flesh or eating and drinking and living in comfort, who will ever see Me face to face. Look at the history of men who have a testimony in matters like this and you will know that in every case that it is only through incessant prayer and fasting that they saw me.

This is the second night of your prayer and fasting vigil and therefore you have crossed the river and are able to see me. I humbly asked; "Lord please when we came here to pray, we did not cross any river. Why would you say we have crossed a river?" The Lord answered and said: "Look, these things are like rivers which separate us and if someone does not overcome them, he will remain on the bank. These things include fear, doubt, weakness from hunger, laziness, carelessness, disbelief, making excuses, procrastination and indifference. These things are like a river that separates us. Whoever shall persevere with self-control, is the one who will arrive home and have good fellowship with Me.

So did your forebears apply seriousness in prayer and had a good testimony. Learn from them therefore and tread their path. Emulate also the examples of the following: Moses who prayed incessantly; Daniel who fasted on many occasions. **Daniel 8:16-19; Daniel 2:16-18; Daniel 7:13-15; Daniel 10:2-7; Jeremiah 1:9; Ezekiel 1:1-6; Ezekiel 2:1-2; Isaiah,6:4-7**; the Lord Jesus who fasted for forty days and forty nights. **Peter, Acts 10:9-11; Cornelius, Acts 10:1-4; Paul, Acts 9:8-9.**

Those who see the Lord face to face are people, who make sacrifices through incessant fasting and prayer. This is the reality. In sum, it is not the one who stays at home who will cross the river on the way to bringing travelers home, but it is the traveler who crosses the rivers, climbs the hills and descends the valleys, who will arrive home and be welcomed and ushered into a place in their midst. For this reason, be patient, exercise self-control and do not be lazy.

Look now, this cloud on which I stand is the cloud on which I led Moses and that generation out of the wilderness. I am leaving this cloud with you in your church, to give you the power you need to ensure the steadfastness of your church. Be, however, warned not to provoke Him to anger so that you do not perish. For the sake of the second death, take good care of yourself because this is the cloud of fire with which I led your ancestors.

While I was listening to these messages, my eyes were focused on the One who was speaking to me; His total appearance. I particularly noted the great brightness surrounding him. I also noticed that on his right was an array of seven stars of great brightness, arranged in two rows. On the left of the One speaking to me was another figure also like a man; and his countenance was that of a man smiling in full appreciation of what the first image was telling me.

He continued, by asking me: Do you see the image of the man who is smiling? He is the Holy Spirit, who represents the Son of Man in charge of you here on earth. He will teach you all things for the purpose of achieving eternal life. For this reason, obey him in all things and do not do that which will provoke Him to anger or that which will make Him miserable. After he told me all these things, the two images, as well as the seven stars and the lampstands, vanished instantly, leaving behind only the cloud on which He had stood but now it appeared as a thick cloud that cast shadows. I was startled and my eyes became clear.

I narrated my experience to my prayer colleague and he, having acknowledged it was the Lord I saw, led us into further prayer to give thanks to God. After this experience, my spiritual eyes and ears were opened, and the Lord gave me a lot of instructions in the form of a message to be taken to the churches. I recorded all the messages in a book as instructed by the Lord, who warned me that I am merely the "message bearer". All these things have come to pass, and I now have the understanding to know that the Lord desires well-being and victory for his saints in these end-time days.

Thus, the Lord Jesus revealed to me the machinations of the Toad, Barr Jessus, and the work of Apollyon, the master of the demonic hosts of the skies, the Dragon and the viper which is the serpent which spits its venomous spittle on the churches. He spoke about all these things and I recorded them for the benefit of saints and any manner of persons desirous of understanding, to obtain realization and spiritual advancement as well as preparing for the end of time with steadfastness and the ability to achieve eternal life.

May the peace, realization and understanding of our Lord Jesus Christ abide with and strengthen all his saints. Amen!

*The 'Bar Jesus' written on the Toad was spelt thus: "Barr with double 'r' and 'Jessus' with double 's'. I believe this was done to show the difference between 'Jesus ' the Lamb, and the Evil spirit.

PART ONE

THE ONE WHO WALKS AMIDST THE SEVEN GOLDEN LAMPSTANDS

CHAPTER 1

THE FIRST VISION:

THE CAT AND THE GIANT MOUSE

In the year of our Lord 1984, on the 20th of November, the Lord revealed Himself and spoke to me, Victor Nyarko Amoah, saying: "You have prepared yourself today to pray and receive the spirit of prayer. But I am asking you to tell me, Victor, how many of you are struggling in the race for the Kingdom of Heaven?" I answered, saying 'Lord, those of us racing for the Kingdom of Heaven are known to you alone.' He asked again, "How many of those of you who gather in your chapel for worship do you think will go to Heaven?" I answered, "Lord, I presume all those who gather for worship will go." The Lord responded: Really? You who are of clay, I will open your eyes and let you see what goes on in your church when members gather for worship. Then my eyes were opened and I saw a very huge animal; a bush cat rolling its terrible eyes. Then I saw a giant mouse and something like smoked fish placed on a brass tray. I also saw that both the bush cat and the giant mouse were eating the smoked fish from the brass tray, taking quick fearful glances as they ate as if ready to escape immediately if anyone approached.

Then I heard the Lord's voice asking me: "Victor, what do you see?" I answered that I saw a cat and a mouse stealing fish from a brass tray. And the Lord said, "What you saw is correct." He explained that the cat and the giant mouse are evil spirits that some members of your church have allowed to dwell within them. The smoked fish in the brass tray represents your faith – that is, the faith or belief of the church members whose faith is being devoured by the evil spirits. Their sole aim is to steal the faith of believers little by little and if they succeed in extracting every bit of it from you, they will afflict you with some evil pestilence in the hope of removing you from the Church or weakening your faith beyond repair. When a member thus falls from his faith due to the wicked machinations of the evil cat and mouse spirits, only the mercy and grace of the Lord can save them.

2. You should also know that the plight of those who have evil spirits in them is more misery. For if they fail to confess to their pastor so he can pray for them, how can the Lord cast out these demons from them? As already stated, the purpose of these evil spirits is to damage the faith of the righteous, by all and any means. Can these people, controlled by evil spirits, ever expect the prize of the Kingdom of Heaven? The Lord is telling you, the righteous members of the church, to keep His commandments and if you do, the efforts of these evil spirits will be frustrated, for the Lord is

omnipotent. Encourage my people with these words.

CHAPTER 2

THE SECOND VISION

THE SPITTING, VENOMOUS SNAKE

The voice of the Lord asked me to look on my left side, and when I did, I saw an enormous venomous snake like an adder or viper. It expanded its throat and opened its mouth, spraying its poisonous spittle on some people. Some of the church members willingly faced the snake and gladly received the spittle, after which they happily showed signs of power given to them by the serpent.

2. This scene surprised me, and the Lord's voice asked me the meaning of this. "I do not know,

Lord" I replied. He explained to me: "This is the agent of the animal that emerged from the sea and has been waging a fierce war on righteous people. This is not the spirit of witchcraft or idols which possess, but that of the Dragon. Those who received the spray of spittle on their bodies are those whose way of life is not scriptural. The powers in the serpent's spittle are doubt, jealousy, seeking vainly for self-respect and complacency, self-aggrandizement, laziness, the habit of reproaching others but refusing to be reproached, becoming angry when reproached, being stubborn or impervious to criticism. Such people are full of negativity; they are eager to teach or correct others but are themselves unyielding and steadfastly refuse correction. These vices are infact manifestations of the evil powers oozing out of the serpent's mouth, and those who are not spiritually aware and watchful will harbour vices within themselves. Pray with the fruit of the Holy Spirit with which you are endowed and pray not with the serpent deeds. Everyone should therefore identify what is in him and pray and repent for the Lord to make you victorious.

3. A haughty spirit is bad. Some people demonstrate haughtiness and attribute their attitude to the spirit of God, but God does not dwell in arrogance and unprofitable teachings. When they were tempted by the devil, they did his bidding and he prevailed. If somebody claims that the Lord's spirit dwells in him, all of you should cross-examine his deeds with the Holy Scriptures. How can the Lord give the strength of healing the sick to someone, and yet he himself remains a sick person? How can a blind person pray for the restoration of sight to another blind man, but cannot pray for his own recovery?

4. The judgment of the Lord starts with His chosen people: the church pastors, leaders and elders for the scriptures say: The Lord will judge His own people. But today is the day of salvation and now

His miracles are available not just for church pastors but also for members. If anybody wishes to do anything in the name of the church, they should inform the leaders, and if they fail to help, the pastor should be informed, and if necessary, the pastor will summon the church elders to pray and the Lord your God shall make everything plain. A way of life will be opened for you to journey on. Hebrews, 13:17.

CHAPTER 3

THE THIRD VISION

THE HUGE TOAD

At the tip of the adder's tail, I saw in a flash, a spirit; it vanished almost immediately into the darkness. Something like a torchlight suddenly appeared in my hand and as it pierced the dark, I saw a huge toad which was the spirit of adultery, impurity and fornication. Its function is to prevent decent marriages and to lure young men and women into uncontrolled immorality and licentiousness. How then can the prayers of young men and women, who cannot control their evil desires, be answered?It is written in the Scriptures that "The time is coming and is already here when true worshippers shall worship the Father in spirit and truth, for the Father wants such people to worship Him." John 4:23 -24. This is the prophecy of the Spirit of Jesus Christ. Many Christians presume that prayers should be said in new languages, but the best and most important thing is that prayers are made in the true spirit.

2. All of you know well that these things are evil and not of God's Spirit: Jealousy, arrogance, hatred, complacency, covetousness, pride and all other such vices. When these vices are in control of a man or woman and they pray, it means that an evil spirit is praying to the Holy Spirit. A worshipper of God should worship Him only in spirit and truth. It is idolaters who worship with their fetishes and in so doing, commit slander, hatred and other vices. In one of His teachings, the Lord Jesus spoke of two people who went to the temple to pray. He said one of them prayed and thanked God for not making him a sinner like "this tax-collector"; the tax-collector also prayed and asked God to forgive

his sins; the second man went home well justified in God's sight. What God likes is repentance and prayers asking for forgiveness. The Lord says, if you can get two or three truthful and faithful persons among you, He will answer your prayers and you will joyously receive what you ask for. Pray therefore in the right spirit and with truth. People who pray in spirit and truth always get the answers they are seeking.

3. Commit these weaknesses to the Lord in prayer: Doubt; Jealousy; Seeking self-aggrandizement; Complacency; Bluffing; Laziness; Reproaching others whilst stubbornly ignoring rebuke; Lies or falsehood; Arrogance; Desiring to teach while refusing instruction, Adultery, immorality and fornication.

I, who was dead, but now alive forever and ever, and I, who hold the seven stars, greet you. Amen forever and ever, Amen. Observe the prayer examples of your forebears.

4. (i) Moses and the burning bush. This very fire was in the clouds and shone in the night. Moses prayed repeatedly; he also fasted frequently. (ii) Daniel fasted and became weak. Daniel 8:16-19, 2:16-18, 7:13-15 & 10:2-7 (iii) Jeremiah, 1:9; (iv) Ezekiel 1:1-5 & 2:1-2; (v) Isaiah 6:4-7; (vi) The Lord fasted for 40 days and 40 nights. (vii) Peter,Acts 10:9-11; Cornelius, Acts 10:1-4; Paul,Acts 9:8-9. Those to whom the Lord revealed Himself are those who sacrificed themselves through fasting and prayer. This is the end of the message. May the grace of the Lord be with you all. Amen!

5. When the preceding revelations were narrated to the church members, some of them started gossiping saying "What numerous revelations are these?" Then the Lord explained to me by asking a series of questions: "Victor, should a father of obedient children continue talking to them? If a child obeys his parents and follows instructions, will his parents continue berating him? It is because I love you that I am sharing this message from the

Lord. If, however, you don't want to embrace it,
you will remain in darkness

CHAPTER 4

SPIRITUAL FELLOWSHIP

Victor, the Lord instructed me, give this message to your congregation. Spiritual fellowship is even more serious than a contagious disease. Anybody who is in fellowship with a congregation controlled by a spirit will also be controlled by that spirit. The devil cooperates with Barr Jessus to entice the whole world and is rapidly marking people with the sign of the Beast **(Revelation, 13:11-16)**. The Lord says that if somebody does not understand these events, then he should sing the song of **(Isaiah 21:11-12)**. The mark the Bible refers to is just like any tribal identifier, or fetish, or other mark inflicted on children and elderly people. If you see some fetish worshippers, you will see fetish marks on their faces or bodies. For instance, worshippers of "Torgbi Dagbi" are called "Dasi: Yewe", etc.

NOTE: A kind of non-poisonous snake called a Royal Python – a beautiful multi-coloured, spotted snake – is worshipped by some people (especially the Ewes in some parts of the Volta Region) as their god. Fetish marks are made on worshippers' foreheads and chins and are called Dasi, designating them worshippers of the Royal Python. Anybody who sees the mark of that snake-god on them instantly recognizes them as "Dasi" In the same manner, worshippers of 'Yewe' (thunder-god) in some parts of the Volta Region and other areas have certain marks made on their bodies that identify them as 'Yewe' worshippers. People believe the 'Yewe' god is similar to the ancient Jewish god "Yahweh" which some Israelites worshipped).

2. The mark of the Beast is spiritual and so not visible. If one is marked spiritually, he will not feel

the pain, and that is the difference between physical marking and spiritual marking. This can be likened to circumcising a male baby or piercing the ears of a female baby on the 8th day after birth. They grow to realize that they have been circumcised or their ears pierced without ever remembering. However, when they witness new babies going through the same ritual, they realize this had also happened to them when they were babies. Their parents know as they will in due course, that the reason for the ritual is rooted in tradition

3. In the same way that spirits mark their followers, so does the Holy Spirit of the Lord marks His chosen people. God chose Abraham and he was given the mark of circumcision and asked to keep the practice going from generation to generation. Genesis, 17:12-13. It was part of the covenant between him and God. 'You shall keep this covenant, both you and your descendants in the future.'

4. Since God's mandates are unchanging, you must know that the circumcision covenant is still practiced. However, the ritual symbolizes more than the removal of the foreskin of every male, Jewish baby and so does no longer exclude women who also share in this everlasting covenant. The Lord confirms this in Deuteronomy, 30:6. "The Lord your God will circumcise your hearts and the hearts of your descendants".

5. This covenant is still practiced by Jews as a symbol of their spiritual affiliation, but the prophecy is manifest in Christ for Christians who believe in Him. Colossians, 2:10-11. Circumcision is different from Baptism. Do not mingle with them, for your marks differ from theirs.

6. As stated, being possessed by evil spirits is like, or even more dangerous than, being infected by a contagious disease. If the fear of the Lord is absent in somebody, he denies His power and you must get away from him. 2 Timothy 3:5. They do not call

upon God when in trouble. Barr Jessus is deceiving many souls and some of these traps are evident in various Bible Fellowships, Prayer Fellowships, and Councils of Christians etc. Those who join such congregations with good intentions who are not careful will eventually lose their good standing as their faith is trampled upon. It is sad because their fellowship with such churches can lead them to destruction. Do not have fellowship with smokers, drunkards, dancers, concert and cinema-goers, idolaters, soothsayers and especially, servants of Barr Jessus. Mathew, 24:5. You must be wary of them.

7. Beloved, any spirit which does not advocate the healing of the sick by His STRIPES, but seeks healing from elsewhere, is not of My spirit. If any of you are sick, you must pray and by His stripes, you shall be healed. Isaiah, 53:4-5; 61:1-6.

8. The fellowship which counsels you when afflicted, to use holy water, incense or employ any

other means which are far from faith in the blood and His stripes, for healing, is the servant of Barr Jessus who is in close co-operation with the Dragon to employ every means at their disposal to drag that person to utter destruction. It tempts a man in different ways or puts adverse ideas into his mind that go against his own gospel and church, causing him to develop a bitter dislike for what he has been taught. The deceived man then starts hopping from one church to another in the hopes of seeing God from a different perspective. This is the power of deceit. The spirit of God directs for the spirit of righteousness, while Barr Jessus is only interested in catching more people to augment his numerical strength. He does not want quality but rather seeks quantity. Barr Jessus presents himself as Christ and deceives people into believing all churches worship the same Christ. It is an illusion for anyone to believe that hopping from one church to another will help them to find strength or overcome temptation. It is only with devoted prayer, humility and obedience, that you will achieve true salvation. If you are sentenced to death in your country and you escape and hide in a territory in the same country, the soldiers there will not stop looking for you until they get you. However, if you escape to another country, you will be safe. "I am born in this church, but the church has no power so let me go to that other church". This is the one in which I am born, so let me die in it no matter how weak it is. Is He not the same righteous Jesus? If you abhor instruction and rebuke and do not seek repentance at your own church, do you think you will meet a different Jesus in the new church?

9. Thus says the One who stands in the midst of the seven golden lampstands and from whose mouth a sharp double-edged sword emerges: "Be on your guard, and do not let anyone deceive you. Many men, claiming to speak for me, will come and say, "I am the Messiah" and they will deceive many people. Mathew, 24:3-5.I am the first and the last witness, the Alpha and Omega. As the son is first

and last in creation, so am I the first and last witness and my testimony is the truth. 1John, 5:6.

10. If you hear that the people of Israel committed adultery, it means they worshipped God and at the same time worshipped other spirits, as was done in Samaria. Anyone who interests himself in visiting other churches must know that he is sharing in their weaknesses too. An example is that the weakness of the Laodicea Church is different from that of Ephesus; so is the church of Pergamos. Therefore, anyone who is going to other churches and leaving his own will have a share in his own destruction and in the long run, will be completely lost. If you are in a red-shirted company, let people see and know you as such, and everywhere you go, you will be identified as one of the red-shirted group. The same is true of white-shirted groups.

11. Every church is controlled by a type of spirit, with its signs, marks and greetings. If a person hops from one church to another, believing that all

churches are worshipping the same Christ, you should ponder over this example. Three men born by the same father have one surname but different birth names. Can the woman married to one of them sleep with all of them as man and wife because they all have the same surname? So it is with spirits. Spirits are called Spirits, but all have different birth names by which they are known. I am holy, so I am known as the Holy Spirit. Another spirit is called "Black Spirit". Another is called White Spirit because it only likes white things even if are stained or dirty, as long as it is white, it likes it. Another is a mixed colour (black and white) spirit. All these spirits have one surname "Spirit". Which of them is your Lord? Jeremiah 2:19.

Those who roam in and out of different churches are spiritual adulterers/fornicators. Anyone who worships more than one spirit is a spiritual harlot when it comes to worship. Jeremiah 3:9; Revelation 2:20; 2 Kings 9:22. You have to examine the spirits and choose the Holy Spirit's Church; that is what the scriptures say. Grasp firmly what is already in your grip.

"Behold; these testimonies are from the seals. Come, I who bear this testimony, urge you to listen to what the Spirit has revealed to the Churches. Be wary. Philippians 3:2-3. I am the Witness, the Alpha and Omega, the Morning star". Revelation 22:16.
AMEN.

CHAPTER 5

JESUS CHRIST IS THE HEAD OF THE CHURCH

At 9 a.m., I heard the Lord calling with a loud voice "Victor, Victor, Victor!" I answered, "Here am I, your servant." Then He asked, "Who is your pastor?" "He is the priest who heads my congregation", I replied. He said, "You have said who he is but that priest is only my servant whom I send here and there. Now tell me, who is your pastor?". "Please Lord, help me," I said, confused. He said: Listen, you child of clay. When it was announced to church members to prepare themselves for the Lord's Supper, some started asking who would administer the service for the Lord's Supper, since the pastor was absent. Some people hoped that he would return before the date of the Lord's Supper while others planned to boycott the service if the pastor was not there to administer it. The best Lord's Supper service, they claim, is the one officiated by the pastor.

2. Deciding to take part in the Lord Supper only if administered by the pastor, does not exhibit the behaviour of a true believer. You must all follow the path of faith. This is a very important message for all Christians to follow. I am giving this message to reinforce and solidify your faith, for Satan and his minions, are employing every imaginable strategy to make you stray from your true faith which will afford him the opportunity to drag you to his side. Will the church member who expects the presence of the pastor before he partakes in the Lord's Supper, not become disappointed and lose hope if the Pastor fails to show up? Therefore, child of clay, tell those members of weak faith to critically examine the scriptures and pray for a full understanding to avert straying from the right path, the Lord says.

3. The one anointed by the Lord is amongst you now. His witness is Melchizedek. Psalms 110:4. If you had understood the scripture cited in Mathew 23:8-10 that you should not address anybody on this earth as Teacher, Father or Leader because we have only one Teacher, Father or Leader – then you have wholesome faith. Anyone who teaches the path of righteousness to others based on the words he hears from God is called Pastor or Leader, for his service is that of a High Priest. One of such people is your church pastor, let it be known that if the High Priest does not endow a person with the power of priestly service, then that person is only a worldly pastor speaking to mortal men and he has no divine authority. The Apostle Paul who was endowed with the priesthood of the Temple testified in 1 Corinthians 11:23-26, thus: - "For I received from the Lord, the teaching that I passed on to you that the Lord Jesus, on the night he was betrayed, took a loaf of bread, gave thanks to God, broke it and said, 'This is my body, which is for you.

Do this in memory of me'. In the same way, after he broke the bread, he took the cup and said, 'This cup is God's new covenant, sealed with my blood.' But the day the High Priest established this exercise, he said: Whenever you drink, do so in memory of Me until I come.' 1 Corinthians 11:23-26. This means that every time you eat of this bread and drink from this cup, you are proclaiming the Lord's death until he comes.

4. Today, Jesus is not on the earth with you physically to serve you the bread and wine as He did when he lived among His disciples. If He were serving you physically here on earth, then you would not be practicing faith. It is written, "the one I am pleased with is the one to whom I give pity and mercy," said the Lord of Hosts. In other words, He has the ability to endow the ones He loves with His power. Paul was not with the disciples when the Lord introduced the Lord's Supper, so how then could he so boldly proclaim: "The teaching I received from the Lord I pass on to you? This

teaches you the lesson that God manifests His power and glory even when all hopes are lost.

5. Examine this divine order, that whenever two or three shall come together and ask for anything in My Name, it shall be made manifest for them. How gracious is it that the power of Heaven is given to humans! It is also provided that what ye shall bind by faith on earth shall be bound in Heaven and that which ye shall lose in faith on this earth shall be loosened in Heaven. Mathew16:19. For this reason, if anyone of you are expecting the pastor, he should rather expect the everlasting High Priest. Hebrews4:14-16. Therefore, anytime you gather for the Lord's Supper, read Revelation1:12-16 and pray to invite the High Priest and it shall be made manifest for you. None should, however, partake in that which is not done in faith. If anybody believes that it is the blessing of the individual identified as a pastor who makes the bread and wine wholesome, let them wait on that human being to do the blessing. Go then and find the meaning of

this: "The horse can be prepared for a battle, but the victory belongs to God." Proverbs21:30-31. Become firm believers and remain steadfast in your faith

6. The Lord said He is the Alpha and the Omega, the beginning and the end. May the peace of the Morning Star, the One who died and is now living forever, be with the church. Amen!

CHAPTER 6

THE SERPENT'S DEEDS

And the Holy Spirit asked me: Child of the soil, what do you think about the scripture in Mathew 7:7:'Ask and you will receive; seek and you will find; knock, and the door will be opened to you?' I replied that it means Christians should ask the Lord for whatever they need on their life's journey and God, by His grace and mercy, will answer them. He said "this is a good reply. Some people among you do not know that they should ask for everything from God and some of your leaders and elders cannot be exempted from this weakness. How can a teacher say to his students that 'I do not know or understand what I have taught you? This is something they do not want to hear. What then is his aim of teaching what he does not know or understand? And how can his students believe or learn the lesson if their teacher does not understand it?"

2. "Therefore if you teachers or priests do not understand something, ask God for an explanation. If you refuse to ask through prayers, then don't teach. All of you should ask and receive, seek and find, and knock so the Lord will open the door unto you. All the names of God are good. They are His names. But the seven spirits of God are in the form of torches, and God is one in three persons. Revelation. 4:5; 5:6. But with humility and obedience, you will receive. Isaiah 30:15.

3. There are some people among you whose minds are still not clear about the spittle being sprayed by the viper on church members; they take it for a mere dream or a meaningless vision. Know, however, that no revelation comes in vain; it aims to help open the eyes of the seer so he can see and

open the ears of the listener to hear more clearly and bring to the mind a deeper understanding; but not those who have refused to pray for revelation, enlightenment and knowledge. They rather accepted the serpent's counsel and so chose not to ask for an understanding of the revelation, because they believe it is just a dream. Some people's faith wavers in these matters and they become seriously disturbed mentally.

4. Let me, therefore, explain the mystery of the viper to you. The serpent is the servant of the Dragon, given to the Beast to use as a weapon or dagger in his battle against the righteous people. Revelation 13:1-2, & 6-7. The power of God is far mightier than that of the Dragon so even if it fights, it will never conquer. The serpent is the servant of the Dragon, so whenever God's people assemble to worship, the Dragon's servant goes there to baffle them with the aim of preventing them from finding eternal life. Its seed is in its spittle and contains all the fruit of man's sin. Galatians 5:19-21. This

scripture points out a lot of lustful desires of the flesh and even mentions that there are more such fleshly desires not mentioned there; it also warns that those who indulge in sins of the flesh shall not inherit the Kingdom of God. These sins, as already mentioned, are laziness, fear, doubt, disbelief, self-satisfaction, self-exaltation, arrogance or pride and the like. These are the seeds of the Adder. Christians should be very watchful and careful about avoiding these vices and become victorious in fighting them.

5. Ask yourselves the generation to which you belong. When John the Baptist was preaching in the desert about the Lord Jesus Christ, the end of the world, the judgment day and God's anger on sinners, many people from Jerusalem and other areas went to him to be baptized, so that they would be free from God's anger. When he raised his head and saw them, with his spiritually opened eyes, he shouted, "You descendants of snakes, who told you to escape from the wrath of God through

baptism, if you fail to repent from the ways of the serpent? I advise you to repent and follow righteousness and you will be saved." Mathew 3:6-7.

6. The Pharisees are also worshippers of God, but the serpent sprayed poison on them. The seeds grow in them and they belong to the serpent fully. In the same way, anyone among you whose way of living is not scriptural is a descendant of the serpent and not of the Lamb. 1 John, 3:7-10. Those who went to John the Baptist to be baptized, were mortal beings so why then did John address them as descendants of snakes?

7. Many people were surprised to hear that a mighty serpent is spitting on some members of the church, but it is very true. It is this same snake that tempted our forefathers in the Garden of Eden; do not deceive yourselves into thinking that it cannot tempt you. Genesis 3:4. This Dragon tempted the whole of Heaven, but I who died but am alive

eternally have conquered it. Revelation 12:7-9.If anyone among you notices traces of the serpent's seeds in him and confesses this to God and begs for forgiveness, he will surely be forgiven. Ask and receive, seek and find, knock and the door will be opened to you. Mathew 7:7.

8. This serpent receives its power from the Dragon and the Beast is Barr Jessus. The Beast also takes its strength from the Dragon. Revelation 13:11-14. I tell you truly that just as the prophet Joel witnessed the coming to pass of God's promises on human flesh, Joel 2:28-29, 3:1-2, sowill it be, in the last days, that people will practice the vices of the serpent's seeds and yet they will continue to worship God with their lips. Mathew 15:7-9. Be careful therefore of yourself so you do not become a victim of this prophecy, for all prophecies are bound to become manifest. The Lord said, in those days, He will pour out His spirit on all flesh and Isaiah also saw that the viper was spitting on people, and when the seed grew it bore adders and

when its eggs are crushed, more vipers are produced. Isaiah. 59:5. God's omnipotence has been immensely manifested in Isaiah 59:1-2 where you are told His hand is not shortened to save and His ears are not dull and can hear your prayers. But during this period, the lifestyles of the children all reflect the seeds of the serpent. Isaiah 59:2-6.

9. It is the very seed that the serpent sprinkles on them that they receive and live on. accordingly, none can be possessed by the serpent and belong to Christ, or His descendants. One bears the fruits of the tree with which he is identified. Oh, a man born of woman, do not make yourself a buffoon or baffle yourself.

10. The consequences of your excessive indulgence in the evil showered on you by the serpent is, that your prayers are not answered, and your handiwork or careers are not prosperous. Isaiah's prophecy has affected you and peace has deserted you. Isaiah 59:7-8. The practice of evil deeds by

those who collected the serpent's seeds, make them cruel, like murderers who have no fear in their hearts. How can you hate your neighbour and yet claim your hands are not bloodstained? Do you not know that whoever hates his neighbour is like a murderer and deserves judgement? Mathew 5:21-22 and 1 John 3:15. Still, the serpent has assigned the Toad, the spirit of falsehood, to entice young men and women to commit adultery and fornication uncontrollably these days.

11. By cunning design, a pregnancy becomes an abortion. Some couples are also lured by this evil spirit and if they do not watch where they are treading, they will be guilty of committing this sin, for many have become hard-hearted due to the serpent's spittle, causing them to terminate a developing pregnancy thus staining their hands with blood. They are inheriting the sin of Onan and worsening their uncleanliness. The hands of young women and young men as well as the elderly, are all bloodstained. Genesis 38:8-10. When their

parents observe them on such wayward paths, they do not warn them, for some of them fear their children's anger when they are rebuked. The question then must be posed, should parents fear their offspring rather than Jehovah?

12. Parents should note that any, whose children's training is not religious cannot escape from this matter. Do not leave your children to the wiles of the serpent. Behold, the serpent is rapidly sowing seeds of evil in your hearts for you to produce more of its kind. These evils – anger, unbridled passion, hatred, bearing false witness, envy/jealousy, are not of the Lord's spirit but rather the serpent's that endeavours to fill you with the seeds of evil.

CHAPTER 7

PRAYING FOR PREGNANT WOMEN

Because of the war waged by the viper, take all pregnant women to the Lord in serious prayer. You will notice that pregnant women usually get angry for little or no cause and even become annoyed with their husbands without provocation. They also pick quarrels when there is no need to do so. People believe it is normal for them to do so and that they will return to normalcy after child-birth. The real explanation of this change is that the viper gets jealous about every growing embryo, just as it got jealous of our Lord Jesus Christ when He was about to be born and was ready to swallow Him at birth. Revelation 12:1-4.When a pregnant woman is imbued with the fruits of the serpent, her heart absorbs these same fruits, and when she gets to term, the baby is delivered through the actions of the heart. The viper thus desires that its very nature be born in the child. Isaiah 59:4.

2. Ponder this mystery: The serpent is capable of mysteriously changing the undeveloped child in a pregnant woman's womb, or even in a weak Christian woman's womb. into its own form. When the child is finally born, it is not like a normal human being. When this happens worldly people send the abnormal child to an ant-hill in the forest where it changes into a Dragon and creeps into the anti-hill. The serpent performs this mysterious change while the unborn baby is still in the pregnant woman's womb, exactly as the colour or the fur of sheep and goats are changed. Genesis 30:37-39. So, you see the Dragon employs all crafty means to make human beings deliver devilish reptiles. Isaiah, 59:5.

3. For this reason, this is what you should do for pregnant women to keep them strong in the Lord. During the first three months of pregnancy,the man should send his wife to his pastor for prayers in his presence, and witness that his pregnant wife is under the peaceful protection of God. Repeat the same process during the second three months (when she is six months pregnant). He can also send her to the church leader or any person officiating at the altar if the pastor is not available. The same should be done during the ninth month before her time to deliver comes.

4. Do not wait until she goes into labour before sending her to your pastor where she will be required to confess her sins. Take all your problems to God in prayer and He will save you. If the Serpent's attitude shows in your lives, you do not belong to the Lamb, and you will be doing only the will of your master, the Serpent, and not God's will. John 8:43-44. The Serpent does its best to make a married couple submit to its will. A wife is

encouraged to deny her husband sexually until her requests or desires have been fulfilled. In homes where the Serpent's seeds are ripe, there is no harmony. The wife refuses to satisfy her husband and perform her wifely duties, the man boycotts meals prepared by his wife and they each pray separately and do not share. In some homes, the man takes counsel from the Serpent to avoid his wife conceiving again, when the child is only a few months old, by spilling his semen after sex or practising family planning. He thinks it is he himself who has conceived these ideas, but no he is taking the serpent's advice.

5. Take note of this then and do not heed the will of the evil one, for if you do, your children's disobedience will be beyond description. Behold, children who are not experienced in life, easily commit deep blasphemy, but when they are asked to pray for forgiveness, they cannot find the right words to express their prayers, so pray for your children that the devil will not overpower

them.Now that you are drawn to the descendants of the Lamb, turn wholly to His ways and laws and do his will so you may obtain eternal life. Isaiah. 8:16-20. Do not go into fellowship with the powers of darkness.

May the peace, might and grace of the One in the midst of the seven golden lampstands and from whose mouth comes a sharp double-edged sword, abide with you. Amen!

CHAPTER 8

DISBELIEF AND SLIP OF TONGUE IN PROPHECY

After all these things, the Lord called and asked, "Victor, Victor, Victor! What are your countrymen saying about the message I gave you for them?" I answered, "Lord, my people are shocked at the message, and some have asked if these messages are necessary for them in this present age; and there was a great disturbance in the church. Consequently, I was seriously rebuked. The majority, of course, do not believe that the messages are from the Lord."

The Lord said, "Look, Victor, I have heard all, and have seen how you have become so sad. I was present when you were called for questioning and even heard some of them say your messages were not from the Lord but from an evil spirit, in order to split the church. If they call the Lord the chief of demons, how much more would you, a worm and one who is like a miscarriage, not be given a more devilish name?

2. They appreciate the presence of the devil in their midst, more than that of the Lord. They, however, do not pray to receive an evil spirit but when they pray for the gift of the Holy Spirit, they expect the arrival of an evil spirit. I have seen how they are still spiritually immature. Why? Are you not aware that the Holy Spirit which delivered messages through holy prophets, is still in existence and is still performing its duties? Or are you not aware that the evil spirits that persecuted holy prophets and righteous people, before the scribes and judges and caused them to be jailed, crucified, or butchered, are also still busy doing their evil deeds? Acts, 4:1-6 & 7:54

3. If they could command and cast out demons from possessed people, as they boldly rebuked you, they would have been perfect in their faith. Can a government be stable if it opposes itself? The scriptures confirm that the Throne of the Lord is firmly established from ancient times and is everlasting. Psalms 93:2. If His kingdom had opposed itself, how could it have stayed strong? All of what you have heard is the gospel truth from the Lord's Holy Spirit, that opens the spiritual eyes and ears of those He examines and finds fit to worship the Lord.

4. Your people have not realized the great change in your mode of speaking. They speak evil against the Holy Spirit, unaware that their hearts reflect the brazen hardheartedness. Their desire is that the worship of God should suit their inward, idolatrous agenda and if that change is not affected, they gossip extensively. Thus, instead of cross-examining the message you brought with the

words of the living scriptures, they fail and fail and never even realize it.

5. But should they continue praying for the Holy Spirit to come into their midst with all its spiritual gifts? Hold fast and remember all you have heard at all times, for this will help to overcome the Dragon and its allies. Keep them in your heart until the time comes. As for your people, they can continue with the plans of their hardened hearts, for they will never be satisfied if they do not act on their hearts desires. Isaiah 8:13-20.

6. Let me explain to you the eruption of major disturbances among your countrymen; a matter that leaves you with a broken heart and a heavy burden. When the Lord's message reached them, some became annoyed with you, some hated you, some feared the exposure of their secrets; others secretly withdrew themselves, while others still feared they would be relieved of their high positions. So, they deliberately behaved as if the

Lord's message you gave to them was new, one they had never heard before. They hold onto the vices of their brazen hearts, claiming among themselves that the Lord's Supper is not pure or perfect. But rather it is their hearts that are filled with impurities.

7. What is the order of the covenant box? It is laid down that only the priests and those who are purified who officiate at the altar, should touch it. Anyone who is not qualified is liable for judgement or even death if he touches it.

8. God is not human, so does not make pronouncements and then alter them. God does not change his pronouncements. When He makes a promise, He fulfils it by all means. Whatever is bound on earth in the name of the Lord, is also bound in Heaven, and whatever is looseon earth is loosened in Heaven. This never changes. It is the offering, which is not perfect that can be defiled, not the altar of the Lord. A similar thing they told

Jesus long ago; that a lame animal offered on the altar cannot desecrate God's holiness, but rather the one who made the sacrifice on the altar should be judged.

9. Behold they whitewash themselves outwardly, but the inside is full of filthy things: favouritism, slander and malicious gossip. In fear of retribution, they speak falsehoods to please others, seeking in vain to find self-respect and fulfill evil desires, like envy and other vices controlled by the power of the serpent's seeds. Mathew 23:18.

10. What is the order laid down for the Lord's Supper? Is it the Altar that is to be scrutinized or to rather examine the offering to be made on it? It is the offering that the priest ought to critically examine before presenting it on the Altar. This is the reason why the scripture instructs that; one must examine himself and not examine the bread before partaking of it. Whatever test the bread is subjected to, one will only find out that, it is

unleavened bread. The Eternal High Priest transforms the bread by His blessed grace. And if the cup is subjected to any examination it is only a sweet wine. The Lord cannot fight with any person who presents himself with a clean heart if He Himself does not come to sanctify the Altar. Whoever partakes in it complies with the right order and righteous is the One who gives the promise and will as well fulfil it. Wherever two or three shall meet in the name of the Lord, I am there in their midst, and by the faith of those who are gathered, the Lord's promise will manifest. Anybody who therefore does these things without faith reaps no benefit.

11. Now, take a critical look at human beings, and you will find that their hearts are full of lies. Man ought to guard his heart more than anything else. Proverbs 4:23. For this reason, it behooves a person to properly examine his heart before eating the bread and drinking from the cup. If two or three ask anything in His name, they will receive it.

If it were not so, then all Christians of the world would be compelled to partake of your loaves in order to be saved. It is not the hand of a human who is blessing the bread and the wine; we have no blessing power. It is rather the mercy and the grace of the Divine High Priest. Once the promise that "Wherever two or three are gathered in My name, I am in their midst", then it is the responsibility of this High Priest, who established the order of the Lord's Supper, to provide the power to transform the bread and wine into perfect spiritual victuals that should provide eternal life; there is no human involvement at all.

12. It is man's duty to examine himself and it is God's grace to pour His blessing on the bread and wine and offer us salvation. The scriptures say that "If your brother offends you, you must go to him and make him aware of his offence against you and settle it with him, for peace. This must be done to avoid a quarrel that will degenerate into animosity. If your brother sees reason and repents, then you

have saved him from evil. Without this, should all Christians worldwide be compelled to partake of the bread upon which you command the name of the Lord, in order to have everlasting life? Know it, therefore, that the power is provided according to the promise, and that, My righteous servant shall justify many with such wisdom. Isaiah 53:11. The shepherd who keeps guard over his flock till the coming of the Lord is more faithful than the one who absconds with a flimsy excuse. Do not be like hired labourers in His service, but just as the Lord Himself sacrificed His life for His flock without fear of wolves, so should you sympathise with and forgive one another; carry one another's burden.

13. Should God's orders and commandments be altered to suit human desires? Is it not the precept of man to discard his heart's desires and turn to God? How does one who is created instruct the Creator to fashion the creation this or that way? Does God Jehovah change in His Heaven, simply because humans distort righteousness and call

falsehood truth and darkness light? Behold, your falsehood cannot alter God. If anyone of you examines himself and realizes that there is bitterness in his heart against a brother, he should settle it with him otherwise, he is setting the stage for a quarrel and fomenting trouble. God's words are not corrupt; nor is the Church of Christ. Know that nothing is sacrilegious, especially when the Lord's name has been invoked, except to you, an individual who considers it so. Romans 14:14.

14. One who consumes the Lord's Supper in faith, shall have the Lord's power manifest in him, for he does not consider it sacrilegious and his heart does not condemn it. So is it written and confirmed and remains an unalterable truth; that it shall come to pass according to one's faith. In this vein, whether the man who breaks the bread or the person who consumes it, everyone must prove himself by discarding the slander of hard-heartedness and turning to the Lord. If you harden your hearts and stiffen your necks, so will your judgement remain in

waiting, you with stiff necks and stony faces.

CHAPTER 9

DREAM NARRATION

And the Lord's voice came to me saying, "Victor, pay attention! Who allowed you to narrate your dreams to them? Is it for you to narrate your dreams or to deliver to them the Lord's message? Look! Whoever has been given My message should deliver it. What has the husk to do with the wheat? Jeremiah 23:28. I answered, "Lord, I thought that by hearing the dreams, they would offer me help in my prayers since the Dragon was fighting me". "Never, Victor, listen. Is it for a messenger to deliver the Lord's message or narrate his dreams? Then I answered, Lord, please, 'I have to deliver the Lord's message, and not narrate my dreams.

Victor, listen now, the purpose of revealing the warfare to you is to give you courage, so that you can refocus your prayers to the Lord to give you victory. Now that you Victor, have exalted yourself and narrated your dreams to them, in search of refuge, are they able to take you seriously and offer you a defence in any sense of the word? You claim to be seeking support from them by narrating your dreams, but do you now realize that it is because of that, that they rather hate you and are anticipating your disgrace and destruction? They never wanted to profit from the message you brought and did not even ask for that. Anyone of them who ask became peeved because it does not suit the brazen image of their hearts desires.

2. Look, they exist for the sake of existence and the coming of the Lord's message to them does not occasion any need to change. The message did not cause even a strand of hair from any of them to

change since it proceeds from life to life eternal. They are however seriously provoked to anger and have risen against you both physically and spiritually. It is the narration of your dreams to them that has brought you all this trouble. This will teach you a lesson, so you know that the sympathy of a mortal man which does not come from a sincere heart is like the flow of tears from eyes exposed to smoke.

CHAPTER 10

DO NOT ADD TO THE LORD'S MESSAGE

Now Victor, answer me with courage. Did I not instruct you not to add to or subtract from the Lord's message? I ordered you to carry the message to them only; you are merely a message bearer. It is not for you to fight on behalf of God so humans will believe in Him and they will embrace you with love. Look! They are all pretenders who stiffen their necks, reposing their trust in the falsehood that they are living in peace and unity, whereas in actualfact they live in animosity and bitter sectarianism. They claim falsely among themselves that there is peace but in truth, there is no peaceful co-existence, how can there ever be spiritual oneness?

2. They claim by faith to be coming to God the Father, God the Son, and God the Holy Spirit; these that are one God, for eternal life. Their unity, as claimed by the church is a mere pronouncement. Spiritually, they resemble a stinking old sore which gets worse every day. Who, in their discord will dress the sore for them to heal in order to hold steadfast to their social unity in order to transform their spiritual oneness into a sweet aroma unto God? They stiffen their necks and refuse to accept the word of instruction because of the brazen images in their hearts. They are never in one accord in any of their meetings.

3. I have warned you about them saying, "never fear them and do not let their presence frighten you. For it is among spiritual novices and people who can't understand spiritual things that you are going to proclaim my words. Be of good courage therefore and ensure that only what you have heard from the Lord should proceed from you. Instead, you took your heart's advice and

wondered why can't these men of divine realization understand these worthy messages. You then trusted in them and later became broken-hearted when confusion and riot ensued. Your heart which trusted them as people of the same spirit failed you when they refused to listen, and you trembled with fear which took your mind off the message given to you by the Lord to proclaim. Your mind and eyes then settled on their rioting and you wished the message better suited their ears. In your isolation and anxiety, you added your own words to the Lord's, telling lies that "the Lord says..." Meanwhile the Lord did not mention any names when He gave you the Altar order which you wrote. Look, the words you wrote with your hands bear testimony against you for telling lies, by adding your own words and causing people to say about the Lord that which He has proclaimed is a falsehood.

4. Look! I, the Lord am God, I am the Almighty. What is beyond my might? The Lord says can I not

accomplish what I plan? Should the Lord continue to speak for the fickle heart to slight and the undiscerning to confuse, in order that rancour and rioting should prevail? Look, all these have happened to let you identify the spirit which is at war with the truth. Note that wherever the truth appears, it is there that evil confuses people's minds to not accept it and repent.

5. Listen now, Victor, if Moses did not fare well for having done what the Lord did not tell him, and did not go unpunished; and Peter also testified about the couple who lied to the spirit of God and died instantly, then you must pay attention: For causing the Lord to be called a liar, your own tongue shall put you in your grave among your people. If you do not take care of yourself and you slander Me once more, that will be the end of you.

6. I have told you war has erupted spiritually and if conquered, it will come physically, and when it does, you must pray, for it is only with incessant

prayer that you will conquer. Your compatriots did not understand, and they took you for an agent of evil. Their faith fought with you at a time that they should be praying to conquer the enemy. It is only by grace that you will have my mercy. Now, you all go and learn about the prophets – from Moses to the least of them, and especially, you Victor, you have been slightly promoted so befriend realization and let understanding embrace you and bring you home.

7. The Lord says about His messages: After the seventh period of the seventh season, His Voice shall be heard again among your natives. Says the Lord of Hosts. Numbers 20:2-12; 27:14; Deuteronomy 1:37; 3:26; 4:21; 32:51; Acts 5:1-10.

CHAPTER 11

THE POWER OF SINGING AND PRAYER

I heard the Lord's voice call and He said: Victor, Victor, Victor: What is the order and aim of singing? I answered: Lord, I know songs must be sung to praise God. The Lord replied: "You are right, but if the Lord does not conquer a war, how can one sing and praise Him?" It is only when God conquers in a war that one can sing and praise Him for the victory. James 5:13. This scripture makes you think that prayers must be offered only in crisis and praises sang only in times of gladness. Only a few people sing in times of crisis.

2. Pay attention! If someone goes before the Lord with prayers and songs in time of crisis, that person is moving towards the perfect might of God and

with persistence, will have access to the total power of God in a short period, because prayer and songs draw the power of God when they come together. It is like the union of a male and female that brings forth offspring. So also does the interaction of prayer and singing in the presence of the Lord deliver God's power. The Lord asked me again. "What kind of songs draws the power of God?" I answered: "Lord, it's only scriptural songs which can draw the power of God. The Lord said, Yes, it is true that there are various types of gospel songs, but the Lamb's songs and prayerful songs draw the Lord's power more than others." The Lord then asked me, "Which religious denomination's songs will you sing when you get to Heaven?" I answered,Lord we shall sing the gospel songs of our denominational churches."

3. The Lord told me: "Be aware that in the kingdom of Heaven, there is no church and a church name does not exist. The selected Heavenly choristers exist in two groups, just as the covenant exists in

two parts. The two choirs exist in one heart, one power and one love and they sing their praise to God in oneness. One group of choristers represents the Old Covenant worship order, belonging to Moses, while The Lamb's choristers represent the worship order of the New Covenant.

4. You who are in the New Covenant era must sing the Lamb's songs. Revelation 15:2-4. I asked the Lord, "Please, which are the Lamb's songs and where can we get them?" The Lordanswered, saying "The hymns of the Lamb abound and are identified by how closely their words are attached to the name of the Lamb, His suffering on the cross and His victory over death. They also allude to the healing power of His stripes, His atonement for the sins of humans in the presence of God and His deliverance of men from sin to eternal life; all these must be sung about

5. Jesus being raised on the cross and His victory over death have a power that conquers the devil

completely. Some of the Lamb's hymns may be found in the GOSPEL MESSAGE, THE NEW SONGS OF PRAISE AND POWER and TABERNACLE hymnals, which you must learn. You need to master the words of the hymns and be able to sing them with a prayerful spirit. If they are songs of praise, you must sing with heartfelt happiness.

6. The Dragon gets very discouraged when the Lamb's songs are sung with clear pronunciation of the words; it gets frightened and flees. Since the devil runs away because of the Lamb's songs, it tries to baffle people into thinking that prayers are only needed in times of temptation and warfare, so when they get tired of praying they give up. Some believe that singing does not matter. Others think that choristers must sing only in competition during church gatherings and in competitions on radio or television, to entertain people. But actually, people are missing the real essence of singing due to the deceptive misconceptions by Barr Jessus, who has deceived people into believing that singing should

have an ulterior motive; to be understood and to be good only in the context of social engagements. Not knowing that, without the power of God, their song ministrations at rallies and gatherings are mere self-exaltation. They are unaware of how the blend of prayer and song are used to draw the power of God. The scripture which says they have the semblance for the love of God but reject His power is manifest on them. 2 Timothy 3:5.

7. Living with this mindset, they quickly rush any sick person to hospitals, where none will require the faith work of prayer and singing to engage the power of God to work. After the enemy gets upper hand and life is lost, they now erect sheds and sing the Lamb's songs, with the understanding of comforting the departed soul, meanwhile, the damage is already caused.

8. You should not resemble them in such actions. If you hear about the sickness of any of your members, go encircle him and sing the Lamb's

songs with prayer and the power of the Lord's arm will manifest.

9. In all difficulty, learn Revelation 15:2-4. andpray that God opens your ears to be able to compose a song with it to sing in times of illness. Do not keep those who fall into the temptation of sickness in the binding of the devil. Pray fervently with the spirit-filled songs of the Lamb to be delivered by the Lord. Take care and ensure that, only the Lamb's songs and the worthy spirit-filled godly hymnals be in your heart and lips. Counsel yourselves with the Psalms which are songs of Moses, for these are songs of praise and guidance. Sing and pray and praise God that the Lamb conquers the devil during times of war. Sing and pray and praise the Lord with gospel songs in your hearts and practice as well. Colossians 3:16

CHAPTER 12

THE EFFECTS OF DIFFERENT SONGS

Barr Jessus captures and conquers people in songs that are not inspired by the Holy Spirit. Some songs sound spiritual but are not inspired by the Holy Spirit. Others resemble gospel lyrics, but the words inspire spiritual weakness. There are still some others that suppress the spirit and adding to a burden of crisis and pushing one further into misery. One who enjoys secular songs always has his faith in God weakened. You have to rise against the devil so that he will flee from you. In most cases, people love to sing songs that reflect the temptations that befall them, and they sing in a manner that lets anyone hearing them understand their crisis and how miserable they are, demonstrating great melancholy.

2. Be aware that demonstrating misery in times of crisis is what the devil enjoys and is his way of making sure you will never set free of him. However, he will instantly flee if he finds that you have changed your affliction to joy with effective prayers and singing. A worthy piece of advice is to consider affliction a joy and not allow it to let you become miserable. James 1:2-4.

3. Therefore, learn spiritual songs and strive to sing them at the right times so that the devil does not trample on you and take you for his prey. A church without choristers and a prayer force is like a city or a kingdom without a standing army to defend it from invasion. Though the Wallof Jericho was mighty, it was razed by the songs of the Lord sang around it, another indication that the Lord's songs, in conjunction with prayer, can break mighty walls. So, even today if you are surrounded by temptation

and foes, singing the Lord's songs through the power of the Lamb will disperse your enemies, for the Lord's might and power are demonstrated through the singing of believers. Hold onto theseinstructions and become steadfast in all things. Don't be deceived by the enemy into slumber, only for him to capture you with no defense. I, the Alpha and Omega, the first and the last witness, proclaim these truths to the churches. Amen.

CHAPTER 13

REVELATION ABOUT HIGH OFFICES

(Can Kings, Priests and Prophets Humble Themselves?)

The Lord's voice came to me saying: Victor, Victor, do you know that it is from the power of the Almighty that kingship, priesthood and prophetic powers come? I answered, please, Lord I know, it is you the Lord Almighty, who enthrones a king and it is you who appoints priests in charge of your duties and it is by your will that prophets exist, to praise, worship and bow down to Your name on earth. The Lord replied, "Son of man, you are right in your answer.

2. Now then, cheer up, son of man, and answer this also. Look! Son of man, from the beginning of creation till now, how many kings have been prophets, while still on their throne? And how many priests have been prophets? I then answered; please Lord, I do not know them all, but I have read in the scriptures that King David was a prophet and King Saul as well. Samuel also was a priest and a prophet. The Lord replied: Son of man, you are right: rare are people who have the spirit of prophecy and have been king or priest, and hardly will a king or a priest become a prophet. Such a one must be able to self-reproach in the presence of his subjects. He is impartial and has the courage to rebuke the wayward without favour or reservation. He should be one who never reverses a decision after taking a vow, even if it affects his interest. For the sake of honour, he will rather, speak with courage and conviction on these issues. When a human receives honour, his heart begins to boast, which is why prophets are not able to consort with

earthly men of honour because the spirits of prophecy submit to one another. 1 Corinthians 14:32.

3. It is extremely difficult for a person to be in a high position and remain humble. Priests and kings ought to submit to God and men, for it is due to God that they are given power. It is only when a King or Priest is sufficiently versed in these truths that the spirit of prophecy can abide with him and guide him, so he does not go astray. Son of man, be aware that the culture of a kingdom is different from the orders of the priesthood and the rules of prophecy are also different. Let therefore the one who is a king, conduct himself in perfect righteousness, and the priest also performs his priesthood duties withoutlet or hindrance, and the prophet also prophesy with total courage. A truthful prophet does not seek honour from people because he knows that the perfect will of God has nothing to do with living in a great king's court and searching for honours.

4. Who can be a king or a priest and still become a prophet? He is the person who will not use his power to accumulate boastful honours and associate with noble names. Look! These instructions as provided in the scriptures are lessons for you to learn so that you do not go astray. The devil, however, makes people obstinate; they do not listen, obey the scriptures and so be granted eternal life. You, therefore, assign guilt when you read some of the examples in the scriptures that call for amendments and claim that if it were you who were tempted, you would have stood firm, but this is the devil's deception. Behold, their weakness has become your lessons for change. If you do not considerthis as a reason to change, but rather judge them, how can you turn unto the teachings? Look! If the living judge them guilty, they are living in spirit in the presence of God. 1 Peter 4:6.

5. It is almost impossible for a Priest or King to be a prophet because a king will probably fear his

subjects more than God and so refuse to follow the Lord's commandments, so will the priest also desire to please his people and for that reversal in righteousness, he will invoke the wrath of God to strike him dead in the midst of his compatriots.

6. King Saul's history and that of other Prophets who defied God's orders, as recorded in the scriptures serve as lessons for you to tread cautiously. It is recorded that King Saul feared the nation and therefore could not do God's will and did not follow the orders of the Almighty. The reason Saul could not stand for the right was his trust in men. The brave generals in his army thought that they could become wealthy instantly by taking the loot of war, to ward off poverty. The king recalled God's commandment in which He cursed the nation and everything therein; the reason that He commanded that everything should be set ablaze. The king warned his generals and reminded them to just follow God's order. The brave generals in whom the king reposed his trust

replied, saying: "Be informed that if you, King Saul will not allow us to secure this precious loot, to make wealth and be freed from poverty, then we will not go with you from hence into war; we cannot continue fighting wars while living in abject poverty, gaining naught. The convention of war is for the victor to possess the loot." On hearing this, the king got discouraged and feared that his mighty generals would forsake him. This fear made the king give consideration to their request and finally, he allowed them to carry on with securing the loot. Bringing along Agag, the captured chief meant that he was in charge of the nation's wealth and where it was kept. He was captured alive so he could show them the depots storing the wealth and was therefore considered generous. He was not killed and was also not considered a captive. The nation longed for wealth and the king trusted his subjects; they all forsook God's will.

7. These are examples for Kings and Priests to follow so they do not trust in men, and caution for

congregations and nations when it comes to longing for the wealth of this world. If our forebears are given as examples for later generations not to go astray and yet repentance is not sought in spite of this, then these later generations will have a worse chastisement than our forebears.

8. The Lamb says, had Sodom and Gomorrah learnt these lessons and heard the voice of the Son of man in the manner that today's generation has heard it, they would have repented and avoided judgement; look! The disobedience of today is worse than theirs. Search the sources of these lessons and remind yourselves and your colleagues that "You are the salt of the world, and if the salt loses its taste, what is it that will substitute it? Mathew 5:13. I, the Morning Star, pray that the Grace of God, the everlasting King, be bestowed on the Israel of God. Amen.

CHAPTER 14

TIME OF PREPARATION FOR WAR AND REFORMATION

Victor, Victor, Victor, having been left in deep thought and fear on realizing the Lord's query of your slip of the tongue, and the rebuke from your people, some of whom even accuse you of possessing an evil spirit, you are seeking consolation. Let me, however, inform you that this is not a time for comfort, but rather the time for girding up your loins and preparing for war. Ephesians 6:10-13

2. Remember that people gave their lives for the establishment of this faith and the worship of God; some were butchered with swords and others were burnt on pyres. Prisons, wildernesses and caves

became places of retreat and succour. Hebrews 11:36-40. They never found comfort in this world until the prophecies became manifest. The Lord Almighty did not forsake them and their souls lived in hope, waiting for the Lord to punish those who persecuted them and how the devil's end would come. Revelation 6:9-11.

3. All those chosen by the Lord who put their trust in Him should have courage, and be righteous in their hearts and have peace of mind, humility and holiness, for His promise says "I will not forsake you, I am with you till the end; thus says Jesus the Lord. This promise is fulfilled and is working in your midst without fail. Mathew 28:20.

4. Hard was the warfare of the first-century faith defenders. The warfare of you end time believers, will be even fiercer, and if the Lord Himself does not descend personally into the war front, all will stray from the truth. This scripture which says If the evil days are not reduced, no flesh shall be saved. It

is because of the chosen ones that all these prophecies are being fulfilled, to make you know the time is due. Mathew 24:22

5. Look! Satan has conspired against all of you living on earth, so be alert and pray that he does not lead you into temptations that will prevent you from having eternal life. Prayer is the light that will shine on your path so that you do not walk in darkness and hit your feet against stones. One who relaxes in prayer is leaving himself in darkness. So do not relax in your prayers. If you pray as is required, then the Lord will shine on your pathways and you will walk in the light of the gospel leading you to salvation.

6. Now Victor, listen! The enemy is in all efforts to provoke the Lord's anger against you. It is out of mercy and grace that He has saved you. Repent quickly therefore in these matters so that you are not charged with them by the devil. The very day you heard the Lord's voice, when he opened your

spiritual eyes and ears, you started considering yourself holier than your peers, whereas no human is righteous on his own; only the Lord. Psalms 143:2; Ecclesiastes 7:20. This is the charge the devil used to let the Lord employ sudden death as a whip against you, that God's plans will be distorted, that people get frightened and refuse to seek after the understanding of the messages. The Lord knows that it is not out of your heart's longing that you slipped tongue. You got saved in tune with this scripture that the sacrifice and the grace of the new covenant have made you inheritors of the eternal life and have atoned for you. Hebrews 10:16-18.

7. Know it then, that it is by grace that you are still alive and do immediate self-renewal, so the devil will be ashamed. While you got defeated by the devil through your self-righteous exaltation and made a slip of tongue, the enemy rejoiced greatly and declared that: Aha! This deserves death and Jehovahcannot alter it because the Lord does not

change His words. The Lord Almighty, having observed that you were to die and your death greatly pleases the enemy; the Lord dribbled him by this declaration that: Rejoice not about your foe's death penalty, so your joy will trigger God's regret to change his mind to keep your enemy alive. Proverbs 24:17-18. Your foe rejoiced about your fall and death but Jehovah reversed it and rather gave you life. Satan got greatly peeved by the Lord's frustration of his plan; he was riled and astonished. His only courage is that; you Victor still hold to your self-righteousness. You need to know, and by hearing this repent and humble yourself in prayer so that you are not ditched by the Lord. This is why I am sent to bring your message of repentance so that you will be alert and the devil would be ashamed. This is the message of remediation for you Victor, proceeding from the work of the power of the blood of the Lamb.

CHAPTER 15

ROYAL PRIESTHOOD

Now then, you take this to the churches and their leaders. Son of man, listen to these: How does this scriptural provision manifest, which says saints are preserved in the royal priesthood? 1 Peter 2:9. Is it about a royal priesthood in this world or the rulership of the kingdom of Heaven?Isaiah 66:20-22. He replied; "It is exactly so, but one has to submit to the teachings of the Holy Spirit and if he ends his journey successfully, then his Royal Priesthood is confirmed. Once the earthly journey has not ended, we are all servants and emissaries of the Holy Spirit.

2. The Lord asked, why then are the leaders of your compatriots enjoying royal priesthood and by that

doing only their own heart's will? They are deceived by their hearts and cannot be saved by the royal priesthood they are enjoying on earth. It serves as no excuse for them to claim they are priests or leaders, for all such big names will not save anyone in the presence of God unless there is full repentance.

CHAPTER 16

TEACHING WITH THE HOLY SCRIPTURES

When I instructed you to tell them to use only the Bible to teach the congregation, you had hardly finished your message when it became a hindrance and a nuisance to them, to the extent that they couldn't understand the message. They never knew that God made you His message bearer. It is imperative to use only the Bible to teach the flock. This is the reason I gave the message to the leader of your people; if he proclaims it should be strictly applied. What is it? Whether they are afraid or being obstinate; none can disrupt God's plan. The understanding inherent in the message is that all the power of God resides in His words, but if you do not read the scriptures, how can the words which possess spirit and life heal you and open your minds to the truth?

2. Be aware that man does not live by what occurs in his mind. Whether it is the voices of the greatest men of wealth in this world or a king with the mightiest power, there is no life but which exists according to the word that proceeds from the mouth of God and His Holy Spirit. Deuteronomy 8:3. For this reason, all priests, leaders and elders must teach with the bible which words are life and spirit, so that hearers will be imbued with the spirit to apply the will of God, so the word will heal them and preserve them for life everlasting.

3. All words in the human mind are dead because on their own the flesh is good for nothing. Words proceeding from God are spirit and life. John 6:63. For this reason, teachers of the gospel should teach straight from the scriptures. Or what do you think? If someone does not submit to the Holy Spirit or someone who does and seeks wisdom from the

Most High, He will give it to them. But if they refuse to pray and go astray, then that teacher will be considered the least of all in the church. Such people should be given time to learn and pray so that the Holy Spirit will open their eyes.

4. Look! Who among you humans on earth have realization and understanding equal to that of God? Look! The wisest man on earth is a fool in the eyes of God. 1 Corinthians 1:20-25. So are the weakness and folly of God stronger than the wisest men. Think of it therefore and know that the wisdom and realization of the wisest human beings do not near the weakest of God's realizations. If your earthly public office wants to engage a manager, will the director not provide the work ethics and orders for him to study and ensure that he will be able to abide by them before his engagement? If the employee is unable to perform, the director has the power to put before him his failures to put him to shame and then rebuke him.

If he deserves to be fired, should he not be sent away?

5. So must you know that this work is far more precious than worldly work. It is the proper understanding and the instructions proceeding from the spirit of the master's teaching that should be offered to employees. Do you not know that it is a serious accounting that this job requires in the presence of the Lord? The case being so, should the master's orders not be used to lead the workers? Therefore, if anyone is to be ordained, he must be given the order book of shepherds out of which he will lead the flock.

6. Many are going to see the message as a nuisance, for their hearts cling to the human being who ordained them into the priesthood. What did Moses do to please God? Was it not the order and laws given him by God to teach that he always used to open the ears of the people? God was well pleased with this action. As disobedient shepherds,

they do not want training and so they will find fault with this message, for they have in their hearts ordained themselves as priests. For this reason, they are unable to submit to the spirit of God to teach them the shepherd's work. Yes! The word reveals that Jehovah has set a stumbling block in Zion. Romans 9:33; Isaiah8:14-15. One who knocks it down will break into pieces and one who finds fault with it shall not stand. This is from Jehovah God, that it is no more Zion alone but wherever God's temple exists. Care must be taken that it does not become a nuisance for you to stumble on and get broken into pieces like the earlier ones. Romans9:31-33.

7. Now, Son of man, answer me. What is the import of the prophecy which says, "The first shall be the last and the last shall be first?" I replied, Lord please, all who have seen the light and have introduced people to it but then turn away from it shall be thrown away and their converts shall remain with the light. The Lord replied, yes, you are

right, but how can one possess the light but have the courage to reject it? That which draws them away from the light is the fact that they have made order and law with their own minds and thus they act according to the will of their hearts and in so doing, stray from the light. Look! They teach but their own teachings do not move their hearts to make them abide by God's word, so how can those they teach have the courage to comply?

8. They fear the humans who ordained them, rather than revering God the mighty Master. They, therefore, befriend hard-heartedness and cruelty; they have lost understanding and realization is far from them. Each rises against his neighbour in his heart, not even knowing that it is the Holy Spirit who protects people in the church so they will not go astray. They consider themselves advanced spiritual men but their obstinacy and attachment to secular wisdom has misled them and they put their trust in the folly-laden claim that "We are in His grace and this is the time for mercy, so God will

forgive." It is true that God really forgives the one who turns away from his sinful path and discards folly, and if the evil one regrets having lived in deceitful ways of the devil and in line with the deceit of the mind and the baffling of the heart. Son of man, obey!

9. Son of man, pay attention. God forgives sins if sacrifices are made for atonement in the presence of God. This duty of sacrifice is for the Lamb, but God does not waste His precious mercy on intentional sins, obstinacy and self-conceit, self-righteousness, self-exaltation, andself-assumption of the deep knowledge in God's ministry. In their private lives, they are captives of folly and are wolves dressed in lambs' wool. In their hearts, deception has made them people of perverted faith. Who are oblivious to the truth and have embraced sectarianism, yet they serve in the royal priesthood over the flock. Jehovah God said: Son of man, take it to those who are in the royal priesthood and force them to desist from such acts

and submit themselves to the Holy Spirit so that they will be able to stand on the day of reckoning.

10. Know that if these sins of obstinacy and folly are measured, then God will also get fed up with having mercy. Jeremiah 15:6. The Holy Spirit will throw you away and your life will end in perdition. Such people are at odds with the scriptures which inspire the church to look to their priests for guidance; those who preach the word to them and see them at end of their lives and teach them faith. Hebrews 13:7. If the lives of priests and leaders do not conform to the word of God, then their portion is shame and affliction. Take care, therefore, to abide by the teachings. You get misled most of the time by your hearts, for which reason you live in folly. Look, who will give praise to that which was properly started but ended in total destruction? So says God Almighty: If someone starts to worship Him properly but later becomes stupid and wayward, God's spirit will never be pleased with

him. Will Jehovah recall the good at the beginning? Ezekiel 18:24.

11. You encourage yourselves with false hopes; that the Lord will accept such a man just because he started well. If so, will the Lord change His words which state that "the sinner should turn from his wicked ways to achieve everlasting life?" All prophecies in the Holy Scripture are pure truth, so it will come to you as you have ended it. He who refuses to listen and repent will see with his own eyes how the Lord will put him among the wicked; yes, you will see how the Lord judges and recompenses the wicked; and for being stubborn, they too will be among them. How will this not frighten you?

CHAPTER 17

THE POWER OF MEETINGS

Who among you knows why Jehovah God gave orders to his nation, Israel to have conventions? It is because He wanted power for the nation. No one should be deceived, Look! Which king well aware of the encampment of enemy forces against him and he does not summon his ministers and generals for counsel as to how to stand firm and achieve victory? Look, the devil has baffled you into winnowing like millet. For this reason, there is a need for you to have conventions and fervent unity prayers. Was it not similar instructions that Simon Peter took when he invited his fellow disciples in great reverence for prayers in a convention? Look, the enemy has deceived you, so your conventions have become ineffective. Luke 22:31.

2. God ordered His nation Israel to have three conventions every year. Look, thrice a year must therefore be an everlasting order for you Israelites and all your descendants, forever and ever. You, who are today's generation, ought to be seen as the chosen ones out of all nations because, according to the Holy Spirit God made Israel His chosen people, Galatians 6:16. Traditional Israel has not obeyed God, which is why He has chosen spiritual Israel so that God can be revered in all obedience and humility; so that they will worship God in perfect truth.

3. Having observed yourselves as God's current Israel, you have to abide by His orders and laws faithfully, for the Holy Spirit has the explanation which proves you are part of the new covenant. For this reason, ensure that conventions are organized,

by all means. If the entire congregation cannot attend in unity, the priests, leaders and elders must be seen to attend three times a year. None of you should be baffled by his heart, to claim that the Lamb has prayed for unification in the name of God the Father, Son and Holy Spirit, to discard conventions. Will the crucifixion of this Lamb, who made such a prayer for His flock prevent conventions for unification?

4. After the Lamb made a prayer of unification for you, would it not be an act of folly to say that the prayer He made for you is of no consequence? What then is your source of support against holding conventions? Tell me now! If you refuse, the unification prayer of the Lamb will be fulfilled by the God of Israel per the promise, for whoever is guided by My spirit cannot rebel against Me.

5. Those who, in their royal priesthood are following their hearts and performing their priesthood duties with obstinate disregard, will not

succeed, and they shall reap the fruits of their own folly. If Simon Peter did not organize a convention, how did they come to know that they have to pray in unity so that the enemy would not winnow them like millet? Just as the Lord Jesus prayed for Peter and the disciples as well as the whole church, so should you also pray for one another and the steadfastness of your faith. Concerning the orders and the laws of the scriptures, recall that when the Lord of the New Covenant came, He did not abrogate any of them, but rather corrected them as needed, indicating that God was not pleased with their sacrifices and offerings. Look! In the Book, it was recorded that I am coming to do God's will. Hebrews 10:7-8. His love, which pleases the Father is the sacrifice He made with His body on behalf of all saints, once and for all. None is, however, found on earth to perform what remains in the order on behalf of the saints on earth. It behoves the saints themselves, therefore, to hold on to the performance of these orders, such as tithes, the first fruits and firstborn of your livestock, as well as the observance of holy conventions. Exodus 23:14-19.

6. Know then that, when you eat the unleavened bread and offer your first fruits and first-born livestock according to the order which remains forever, so should you also know that your conventions which you shall call holy meetings for God, also remain forever and do not forget the other rituals, which also remain forever. For this reason, make sure you organize holy conventions thrice a year. This is the order for God's Israel. Leviticus 23:1-13. This is the order for conventions according to the Old Covenant. In the New Covenant, the Lord does not burden you with any orders except that you follow instruction to convene holy conventions three times a year. Deuteronomy 16:16-17. Look! All commandments given to the nation by God, are taking effect in spirit in the order and power of the New Priesthood, so when saintly priests meet, it appears

in spirit as the Holy Convention of God. Do this so that Jehovah will bestow his spirit on you perfectly.

7. Look! Anybody who considers these issues frivolous is driving himself into darkness and inviting judgement, for these are the lessons that satisfy God's heart. Whoever rejects them destroys his soul. Proverbs6:23. If they disobey and reject God's instructions, remaining obstinate and rancorous would remain accursed by raising their hands in divisiveness and sectarianism. If the inference is made that they are Godly men raising holy hands against obstinate men of folly who also claim to raise their hands and proclaim God's blessing, after church service, and they prevail, all will come to naught.

8. When the viciousness of obstinacy drenches them like dew, and the congregation under such pastors become wicked and refuse to pay tithes, then the Holy Spirit picks out the obedient ones from among them and places them under faithful

pastors. Before long, their churches disintegrate and collapse. Such priests and their households must then search for another means of livelihood and pangs of hunger cause them great discomfort because they abandoned the work of God. Therefore, whoever considers himself God's Israelite among you should submit himself to the teachings of the Holy Spirit. Look! Turn unto the teachings and unite in meekness and affability and see if I will not shower my spirit on your church in abundance. Proverbs1:23. Look! God's prophetic spirit and the power of divine healing are like water springing from a fountain on a mountain rock. Judges15:19-20. The fountain from the mountain rock flows, running into the valleys to water the fields. It runs through forests to feed herbs and flowers so they can provide sweet fragrance in the fields and the valleys. Forests are fed by the same water so that their trees can grow, and their branches provide shelter for the birds. The trees will also bear fruit in the right season and even when they age, they remain fresh. Psalms92:14-15.

9. While the Spirit of God flows like a fountain and some trees are on high ground the fountain flows but is unable to water all the trees to bear fruit, at the right time. Thus, as the fountain flows downwards, it makes pools on low-lying ground. In time these pools overflow further afield, flowing beyond high ground and feeding low lying ground. Such fountains also flow near human habitation and feed people who drink of their waters and are comforted and enlivened.

10. Therefore, whoever submits himself on hearing the gospel, is given the power of prophecy, of healing, of casting out evil spirits, of meekness and an understanding of spiritual matters and the realization by the Holy Spirit for the advancement of the church of the Lord. The Holy Spirit cannot fellowship with someone who hears the gospel and does not submit and instead, is boastful.

11. Anybody who desires the spiritual powers bestowed by God's grace should be lowly in heart and learn to be humble so he can find solace in his soul. Rulers of royal priesthoods learn from Me forever. I am the Morning Star and grant you the courage so you may hear me when I say to you: "Learn priesthood in the right way from Me. May the Holy Spirit give good testimony about you". May the peace of the Lamb abide with God's Israelites forever and ever. Amen.

CHAPTER 18

THE PROPRIETY OF WORDS FOR TEACHING AND REPROOF

The Voice sounded in my ears from midnight till dawn and I recorded it as a testimony for the alertness of saints. I heard the Voice say: Victor, Victor, Victor, son of man, which loving father would find his child involved in a vice and not rebuke him? Which child is it, who guards his way in truth and righteousness, and yet his parents continue to reprimand him at the top of their lungs in the neighbourhood? I answered, please Lord, any father who loves his child warns him for his betterment and the parents of every obedient child are pleased with him, but the notorious child who does not obey is always chastised by the parents, to repent.

2. If this is so, then take it to those who are gossiping, saying "Enough of these claims of prophecy, that God says this and God says that, with so many words of rebuke, that it is clear that God's word of prophecy says that people should be reprimanded and seek repentance. If they do not want to hear the rebuke of God's prophetic spirit, then they should simply guard their lifestyles and turn to the truth in their hearts, so that Jehovah does not put them together with the evildoers. They will then be free from rebuke. You would have been close to perfection if you had understood that "God rebukes the one He loves". Hebrews 12:5-6. And since you do not understand and you do not know God's favour towards the one who accepts rebuke, you all strive to avoid rebuke. If any of your actions deserve rebuke, you make efforts to find some excuse for it, to prevent rebuke and so you tell lies in doing this, and

thereby seeking refuge in lies and acrimony, just to avoid rebuke. If the Lord is to keep speaking on such matters, the living truth is that "If someone does not accept rebuke to mend his sinful ways, such a one does not deserve my fellowship".Isaiah 48:17-19.

3. It is proclaimed that "the raging whip will destroy the refuge of lies". Isaiah 28:15-18. If the prophecy is fulfilled to destroy the refuge of lies and yet you seek refuge in lies, will you not be destroyed by the raging whip in addition to the spirit of lies? Learn therefore to be truthful in all matters. Even in your periods of rebuke, speak the truth for the sake of repentance, for God penalizes the child He loves as a way to reformation by correction. 2 Timothy3:16-17; Revelation 3:19. If the Lord advises you to repent but you dodge reproof and instead seek refuge in lies, hardening your hearts and refusing to change, then you surely deserve punishment. But the Lord's corrections don't come only in punishment but through rebuke as well. What will

be your refuge on the day of chastisement? Whoever relies on falsehood and runs away from rebuke will find no peace with the Lord. One can be free in the sight of men, but the chastisement remains firm in spirit.

4. Be aware that those who have been chosen to avoid being judged together with the world, are those who are under present-day rebuke and chastisement, to get them prepared for judgement day but if you refuse to repent, you will forever remain without messages of correction and rebuke. Instead, you all will be gathered together till the judgment day of the world. There you will remain in idleness as if in peace or solace and destruction will come to you suddenly and there will be no one to save you. Do not be astonished if you find sinful men living in peace without punishment, for the judgement of such people is in tandem with that of the world. God is not bothered about them, for they have been marked for judgement, together with the world.

5. Do not, therefore, be happy if you do not receive any punishment for the sins you commit, but rather be happy when you are judged and rebuked, so that when the time for the judgement of the world comes, you will be seen to have prepared already. Look! Be alert about this. 1 Corinthians 11:31-32. If God prepares you with chastisement alone without rebuking you first, your bodies would be torn to pieces and become worthless. Since you have not changed, God has also chastised. Look! Chastisement is for the kind of sin that should not be mentioned among you, that the Lord has seen. Dare you disclose it to them and see if they do not quickly seek refuge in lies? Look! The Lord's whip is already raging on the wind. What then is it? Will the Lord be pleased with such a nation and such a church?

CHAPTER 19

FORNICATION, ABORTION AND VOWS

Your young men and women revel in wild fornication, having been encourage by the viper and the spirit of the toad, which has empowered them to enjoy on a daily basis, the type of sin committed by Onan; they eat of it like it was food and drink. It is their own blood that they spill through the lust of fornication and by taking birth control pills and using condoms; they are like Cain. Look! The blood clots are discarded and all those souls spilled through fornication and washed away with water, are wailing into the ears of the Lord from the earth and have become a boiling cup of wrath in the eyes of the Angel of the Lord. Look! If they do not repent, they will drink of this cup and see its empty base. Will the Lord congratulate them for such lifestyles? Psalms 75:8.

2.The adults whose lives should serve as examples for them to emulate are even worse. They use drugs, if for healing there may perhaps be some understanding, but rather for the destruction of life in the womb. Some of them have found that consuming sweetened items such as sugar mixed with a blue powder and other ingredients by pregnant women, will induce miscarriage; giving a reason that, the child is not grown before another conception. When such poisonous drinks make those who take it fall sick, they come to ask for prayers, claiming that the devil is tempting them. Will God's anger not make a query?

3. Those of them who pretend to understand and do not apply drugs get into unending arguments, resulting in quarrels and hatred among couples because the wife is denying her husband because the child is not grown enough for a new

conception. The devil caused them to fall into temptation and because they are unrepentant the enemy has the chance to attack them. Will Jehovah save such people in their hardheartedness? If you yourselves allow the devil to take control of your body which is destined for death, then your bodies have become weapons of uncleanliness. Look! That which grieves the Holy Spirit is when couples deny each other not for good reason but cruelty. Woe unto those who do such a thing because they have given way to temptation and allowed it to stand between them. Woe unto wrath mongers that the prophecy which says, it is better than weight is hanged on their necks and they are thrown into the depths of the ocean, is not manifest on them. Mathew 18:6-7.

4. For this reason, anyone who commits this intentional sin, for which oneself or one's child falls sick, should not tempt God. By hearing this call, all that you need to do is to retreat from your sinful path and repent. Or, what do you think? Your

forebears were given an order as to how to vow to God, and this vow requires humans to set aside days to make themselves holy for God. Numbers 6:1-8. What days do you set aside for making yourselves holy as a vow to God? What do the scriptures say? It is written that couples should not deny each other, except that the two agree for a time for prayers and should come together after that, so as not to be overcome by the devil 1 Corinthians 7:5. Should you let yourselves loose until sickness befalls you before you turn to prayers?

5. Is it not peaceful, if a couple whose child is not yet grown practice abstinence and use this period for a vow to God and make themselves holy unto God in prayers, rather than indulging in fleshly intimacy? This practice of cleanliness will save them from many cunning ways of induced abortions. Truly, this nation does not know how to prepare and keep their bodies clean for God to courageously move among them!

CHAPTER 20

HOLINESS AND THE SPIRIT OF DECEIT

Even for their fasting prayers, they do not know that they have to set aside at least 3 days to abstain from intimacy before getting into it. So also, during the time of the Lord's Supper, they continue in their fleshly intimacy and so are not able to remain healthy spiritually. Exodus 19:14-15, 1 Samuel 21:5-6.

If there are some among the chosen, who blemish themselves and mingle with you at your "meals of love", have they not then defiled their souls in the presence of the Lord? If they are able to be deceived into taking part in their lewd acts, then they are just like them.

2. People with lewd lifestyles roam from one church to the other and if any of the churches they visit are under Barr Jessus, they realize that their way of worship is different from the true worship order. There are certain things that are not needed in today's true worship, but they are misled into practicing these rituals at these services. Such people believe that what they have discovered are things which render their services perfect. All that which the Master of the New Covenant did not do, and did not teach anyone to do are not needed in the New Testament worship. Hebrews 8:7.

3. The question is; "Lord, what should be done to have eternal life?" The answer the Lord gave did not indicate that drumming and dancing draw anyone to perfection. The role of drumming and dancing in almost all churches is from the spirit of unrighteousness, which is Barr Jessus. Look! God does not desire for His people to drum, dance and clap hands but rather to tread the path of holiness with a renewed conscience in the Lord Jesus Christ.

1 Peter4:9-11. Drumming in the name of God was done by King David in the Old Covenant but never near the worship of the Altar. The one who is greater than David came and having got close to the righteous way of salvation, He realized that living in this world is all about warfare. Job 7:1; Luke 24:46.

4. He, therefore, proclaimed: "My soul is trembling into death," In other words, that, which He considered and had the understanding of, is that there is no victory in drumming and dancing. This is the reason He did not include drumming and dancing when He established the New Testament order on earth; but rather prayed until His sweat turned into blood falling on the ground. What befell humankind requires that one must fight and win, and this has nothing at all to do with drumming and dancing. Revelation12:17; Ephesians 6:12. Having been established that the Lord of the New Covenant considers living on earth a battlefield and so did not establish drumming and

dancing but rather went with tears and wailing before the One who raised Him from the dead, and in expressing the trembling of His soul, should we not take instruction from the scriptures which says "Employ reverence and trembling in your salvation work? Hebrews 5:7.

5. Jehovah does not demonstrate His power through drumming and dancing. Drumming has become a demonstration of the power of Barr Jessus, for it is when doing this that he enters into their midst. His arrival is taken for the arrival of the voice of Jehovah and the spirit of the Lord Jesus. It is not by clapping hands that the spirit of God will embrace you. He is not deaf, or unable to hear. Watch your iniquities and repent and Jehovah will turn unto you, says the Lord. Isaiah 59:1-2; Amos 5:23-24.

6. If anyone should hold to the understanding that his health and the remission of his sins can be realized through any means apart from the blood

and sacrifice of the Lamb, then that understanding comes from the unrighteous spirit, Barr Jessus. This spirit is actively at work. All captured by him live in an unrighteous worship order but claim God with great courage as if they were righteous. If their zeal in night-long services and fasting prayers were applied to their lifestyles and marriages, they would be closer to perfection. The unrighteous spirit, Barr Jessus, does not allow them to do this. Let them not baffle you with the size of their names. Identify them by their fruits. 2 Peter, 2:1-3.

7. Is it not the One who gave the law, "Thou shall not commit adultery" that also commanded "Thou shalt not steal?" Now, if you are not a thief, but a polygamist, how can you be righteous before the Lord? Look! Jehovah has not created anybody for perdition. Certain fellowships, however, separate their members from God by their actions. They proclaim God with all their might, courage and confidence but their actions lead them astray. Their fellowships have become those of Satan and

darkness; Barr Jessus is their courage. He has deceived them with the name of Jesus to believe him to be the Lamb identified by God for the salvation of the world. If you fellowship with them, you will also share in their punishment. 2 Peter 2:12-14. The end is near, so must the devil's hidden agenda be exposed for the correction of the chosen.

CHAPTER 21

CARE FOR HAIR AND CLOTHING

Look! If you expect a timely reply to your prayers, then take good care of your bodies. Men must cut their hair to avoid long growth and let it be kept in good form. 1 Corinthians 11:14. Women, with long hair, must cover their heads with neat headgear to avoid creating a nuisance for the holy angels who are fighting in your defence for salvation. 1 Corinthians 11:5-10. Long hair left flowing becomes a trap for Angels and since Barr Jessus is well aware of this, he advises a woman to expose their long hair for the admiration of the eye. This has become fashionable in today's world of mundane desires.

2. If you are a woman and you by your own understanding, refuse to cover your hair while you

pray, you have become an agent of Barr Jessus, working to deter angels. Barr Jessus does such things through women of high positions whose long hair is a trap for Angels. 1 Corinthians11:10; 1 Timothy 2:9. If an angel is bringing the answer to your prayers and He approaches to meet a nuisance and a stumbling block, will he have the courage to come with the reply? You are surprised of what I have told you about angels but be aware that all the might and power of God exists for those who comply with His orders.

3. If you have ever read in the scriptures, how the Angel of God fought with the agent of Barr Jessus, for the answered prayers of Daniel, you will not then be surprised. Daniel 10:12-24. Look! It is always so that Barr Jessus and his agents are at war with Jesus, the Root of David and His Angels. Therefore, do not use your bodies as weapons of uncleanliness, but rather weapons of righteousness in support of Jesus, the Root of David. You will

thereby put to shame Barr Jessus, the unrighteous spirit. James 4:7-8.

4. Now, let me teach you the type of creature this Barr Jessus is and where he comes from. Pay attention, therefore to all that is coming. Barr Jessus was an angel that used to walk in front of the Lamb and accompanied Him wherever He went. He was therefore privy to all the ways of the Lamb and almost all His mysteries. He was a morning star of great righteousness and was therefore considered in Heaven as a begotten son of the Lamb. There exists a reserved post for the children of the Father and those of the Son, respectively.

5.Barr Jessus fell into the hands of the Dragon, who conquered the morning star in him and drew him into his warring fold. Revelations 12:3-4. The Dragon took control of him and gave him all his power to battle all of you who dwell on the earth, you for whom Jesus the Lamb has a salvation plan to save as his own descendants and children. This is in fulfilment of the scripture which says; he shall have descendants for the efforts of His soul. Isaiah 53:10-11. Now, if His soul labours for you and you by your own villainy destroy this ready-made path to salvation, you will be likened to the folly of Esau, who offered his birthright for sale. Be alert therefore that none sell off their birthright. Hebrews12:14-16.

6. When the morning star fell at the hands of the Dragon, he introduced himself on earth as the son of Jesus Christ, hence the name Barr Jessus. Despite his claiming sonship to Jesus, all its actions are at variance with the will of Jesus, the Christ. His unique aim is destroying the work of the Lord. It is a spirit that dwells in humans and if one in whom Barr Jessus dwells dies, he goes on to possess another. Once possessed that person tempts the Holy Spirit. In the present era, this spirit has invaded worshippers of God rapidly, by confusing

them with his name, as if he were the Christ Jesus. Mathew 24:23-25.

None will be able to escape him without the grace and mercy of the Lord unless the specially chosen ones, who by their faith and long-suffering, maintain their righteousness and repose with total trust in the Lamb. These are approved by the Lord to be given realization and understanding to be able to overcome the enemy; a vicious, unrighteous agent. Oh, human beings, how are you going to differentiate between Jesus Christ and Barr Jessus? It is only by great mercy and grace that the difference is revealed to you, so you can identify the difference and avoid submitting to him, for all his mode of worship is uncleanliness and filth and fighting over the sanctuary. Mathew 24:15-16. Flee, therefore, from all these filthy things, in order to secure eternal life.

7. Son of man, you were astonished when I told you that, the place preserved for Satan is the Abyss but

since this place is frightful, he fled onto the earth, tormenting saints and fighting to baffle all men, to lead them astray and rule over them. Son of man, do you know where he has mounted his throne? I replied Lord, I read in the scriptures that, Satan is the King of this world. The Lord said: Look! It is Satan who made himself King over the world, but it is not the Lord Almighty who desired it. It was man Jehovah ordered, in the beginning, to rule the earth and dominate it, as well as the oceans. Genesis 1:28.

8. Dragon is forcefully fighting with men with the aim of conquering them and mounting his throne among them, Jesus has not allowed him to achieve. For this reason, he has established his throne with all his power and might, under the oceans. It is from there that he teaches idols, evil spirits and Heavenly spirits and even human beings, his evil ways. He gives them all his powers to fight men on earth and even to fight the Heavenly hosts. Revelation 13:1-2, 19:19.

9. Thus an Archangel from among the heads of our nation fell from the sanctuary and to the vicious host of the Dragon and became an angel of the evil one. He is the one the Dragon sent into Hades to draw souls into the Abyss. Jude 5-6. When the Lord Jesus died, he used all his might to release almost everyone from Hades, which is why those in Hades are only a few. 1 Peter 4:5-6. Since those in Hades followed Christ, Satan let the evil agent in Hades wage war and change its evil designs to look like the Lamb's, but is actually the agent of the Dragon, namely Barr Jessus. Revelation 13:11-12.

10. The reason Jesus is named King of Kings and Lord of Lords is that, he has conquered the Dragon, the Beast, the Great Whore and the man of sin in Heaven, and when he descended to earth, he again conquered the man of sin. Christ, by walking on the sea rendered the throne and powers of the Dragon, His footstool. This is where the Dragon has undergone great subjugation, for the prophecy declares: Sit on my right hand until I render all your

enemies your footstool. Psalms 110:1. Christwalking on the sea is the same as you, walking over your enemies and trampling them. Look, so has Jesus the Lord given unto you and to all believers, the power to step on serpents and all the powers of the enemy without you suffering any defeat, says the Lord! Mark16:17-18; Luke 10:18-19. Therefore, when you cast out demons, command them not into the sea but the bottomless pit, for in the sea, they get empowered to come on earth and fight you. In the bottomless pit or the Abyss, it is extremely difficult for them to return and give you trouble.

CHAPTER 22

THE DRAGON, THE BEAST AND THE HARLOT

Son of man", from where come these names in the scriptures such as the Dragon, the Beast and the Great Whore? Who made them and where are they going? I answered, please, Lord, I know nothing about these. The Lord replied, really, son of man, you can't know, for these mysteries have been sealed and unless the seals are removed, none can know. Even though these mysteries have been revealed to some prophets, they were not allowed to divulge it because it has been sealed and kept hidden. Daniel 12:8-10.

2. Listen, Son of man! All these names such as the Dragon, the Beast and the Great Whore, have a unit head which is Satan. These were created by

God as leaders of a host of angels. The first is the Dragon which is a snake of two types. The Dragon is depicted as a coiled snake and is of separate power. The flying Dragon, which goes on wings, has different powers and might, and the Dragon that is the ancient Serpent, has different powers and might. Isaiah27:1; Revelation 12:3-4. When the morning stars,head of the angels fell from Heaven, it became Satan.

3. These are the powers Jesus conquered when he walked on the sea. It was not the ocean that the Archangel fought within the sea but rather the power bestowed by the Dragon's throne which you thought was an encounter of power with power. Revelation 16:3. Satan the Dragon was an Archangel on the Mount of Congregation, but he exalted himself against Jehovah, the Great King of our nation and for this, was thrown down from the Mount of Congregation onto the earth.

Arriving on earth, he never found solace and therefore went to establish his throne under the oceans, with the aim of capturing all humans so as to let his kingdom dominate the earth. The Beast is also a fallen angel but was not an Archangel, and he, having been conquered by the Dragon, is so named. This vicious agent of the Beast, which is baffling men on earth, is Barr Jessus. This Beast designs its ways to look like those of the Lambbut following this path leads to deception and perdition. This Beast has sent false prophets into the world and thus reveals himself as an agent of light and by so doing, is able to lead many astray. Its name nearly simulates that of the Lamb of God.2 Corinthians 11:13-15.

4. The ruler of the kingdom of demons is the Dragon. Angels who are unable to hold onto righteousness fall under his domain. Angels of less might who stray are given power by him and are classified as the Beast, for they use humans as their support to be able to accomplish their plans. They

receive orders and commands from the Dragon. These fallen Angels are able to deceive kings, great men of honour and priests, who are led to treading the path of the Dragon's kingdom. Humans who receive power from fallen Angels to capture souls are referred to in the spiritual realm as whores. Humans thus conquered, have been used, according to nations and languages and the rivers of the earth to conquer an uncountable number of souls. Revelation 17:15. The agent of the Dragon ruling in the air is called Apollyon and it also comes from the Abyss to fight saints on earth. Revelation 9:11.

5. Your mind is now clearer about what I told you previously; that Jesus walking on the sea is a triumph of power. By walking on the sea, all rulers and power established under the sea become the footstool of Jesus the Lamb, and he has triumphed and trampled over all of them.

6. The Dragon has subdued many mighty merchant vessels, sailing on the sea to its worship and libations must be poured seeking permission from the Dragon to enable vessels to sail in peace. This phenomenon prevails today but Jesus the Lord has given faithful believers power over the Dragon and all of its powers. Because of this, Barr Jessus is peeved for he does not want to be trampled on by anyone. For this reason, he has deceived many into mixing sea-god worship with the worship of Jesus the Lamb. They would, by all means, either worship at the seashore or fetch the coastal sands or fetch seawater to ensure that the sea plays a part in their worship. They in their ignorance turn to worship what has been put under their feet. The scriptures, therefore, are manifest when they say, "it is not all who proclaim me, Lord, who shall inherit the kingdom of Heaven. Mathew 7:21.

7. The Dragon draws wayward angels into the power of his kingdom under the sea and gives them rules and orders which these agents then send to

the leadership, kingdoms and priests on earth, convincing them to apply the rules of the Dragon when governing their institutions. The kingdom of the Dragon, therefore, extends from under the sea to cover the earth. Revelation 16:13-15.

8. Look! All the visions Daniel had, are about the end time. Daniel 7:1-28. All these messages will be clearly understood at the end time. The Beast is represented by humans possessed by wayward angels who have power from the Dragon; kings, great men and rulers on earth. All who worship the Beast and its idols will reap their reward in the lake of fire. Daniel 8:1-27. This is where the separation of goats from sheep is manifested.

9. The ram with two horns represents the New Covenant worship order of Jesus the Lamb and the billy goat are indications of how people of the end time will by their hearts and earthly traditions, collapse the order of true gospel worship. They will draw worldly rulers and their culture into the

worship order of God. This will persist to the extent that the true order of worship will be subsumed, for it is written that the latter will defeat the former. Daniel 8:5-12. So will the worship of earthly gods, culture and idolatry as well as the festivities of earthly kingdoms mix with the worship of God, so they will become defiled like in former generations. Mathew 15:5-6.

10. The whole world will be confused by this mode of worship, as earthly culture and the culture of Christ intertwine with one another. This occurred in former generations and all went astray. 2 Kings 17:33-34. So does the Dragon continue to baffle the world with his wily ways? These are the ways of Barr Jessus, the unrighteous spirit. Look, straighten up and be alert. Will Jesus the Lord find any righteous ones on earth on His second coming? If you find this mixture of worship in the heart's sanctuary of men is correct, then the awful horror has entered the sanctuary, where it ought not to be.

11.Barr Jesus is making every effort to alter the worship of God and change it to idolatry by building shrines and erecting totem poles in the form of the crucifix which some bow to in worship, claiming it is a symbol of Christ, the Lamb of God. The commandment says Do not make any image to bow to. Leviticus 26:1; Deuteronomy 4:15-16. All actions of Barr Jessus are like those of Christ the Lamb unless one is aided by the Lamb to differentiate between them. Revelation 13:11.

It has two horns just like the Lamb, an indication that its orders are fashioned like those of Christ, but its voice sounds like the Dragon's voice, which means that its fruits are far at variance with the scriptures. Marriages are conducted anyhow, with two or more wives permitted, thus covering their adultery. Women are permitted to become priests and leaders; these are evil practices. Revelation 2:20; 1 Timothy 2:12-15; 1 Corinthians 14:34.

12. Delivering souls for Christ through adultery is a deception that draws the soul to Barr Jessus; such people cannot please the true Christ. Look! Barr Jessus is thus deceiving the whole world and binding them in chains for the Dragon. This unrighteous spirit of Barr Jessus possessed men of this world in the past and used them to fight against saints. Acts 13:6-10. At present, the Dragon, the Beast and the great harlot, are collectively devising ways and means to assemble all the nations of the world to fight a fierce battle with the Lamb and His chosen saints. Revelation 19:19-21.

I am advising you accordingly, that you all must make great effort to be on the side of Jesus the Lamb so that the sharp sword coming from the mouth of the One on the horse does not find any evil in you and take you to the second death. I, the truthful witness, say these things, so look and be alert. Revelation 16:15. Amen!

CHAPTER 23

DUTIES OF PREACHERS OF THE GOSPEL; OVERCOMING SIN; HADES AND ABYSS

I, Victor Amoah heard this voice sounding loudly in my ears saying; "Write them down for remembrance." I hurriedly took an exercise book and recorded the messages. What the voice said is exactly what I recorded. The voice called me three times; Victor, Victor, Victor, what does it mean when I say one's blood will be visited on someone, or that the blood of all victims will be visited on the murderer?" Mathew 23:34-35. I answered; "Please Lord, for one's blood to be taken from his neighbour or himself, means that the murderer deserves to go to Hell. The Lord replied; Yes! This is true, but since you know that a murderer cannot

enter the kingdom of Heaven, you mentioned Hell.
Let me counsel you that there are many types of
sins that lead to the visitation of blood when one
commits them. These include murder, hatred, libel,
adultery, fornication and uncleanliness but more
particularly murder, followed by adultery and then
sins of the tongue. Mathew 5:21-22; Ephesians
4:29. It is for the sins that do not lead to the second
death that you should pray for.1 John5:16-17. If
one is taken straight to Hell, without judgement or
probing, then blood is visited on such a one.

2. "Now then, son of man, show me the difference
between Hades, the Abyss and the Bottomless Pit
and Hell. If you know this, then say it quickly!! I
replied: please Lord, what I know is that Hades, the
Abyss, the bottomless pit and Hell are places of
affliction. The Lord replied "You made a good
attempt on this one also but since you are flesh and
blood, you cannot have a good understanding of
this. Look! The understanding of all these mysteries
came from the removal of some seals by the Lamb

and I am given the authority to explain them through you for the comprehension of humans and for the power of steadfastness on the day of judgement.

3. Look! It is because you don't understand what Hades, the Abyss, the Bottomless pit and Hell mean, that it is difficult for you to accept my words of counsel. If you ever understand the affliction behind these names, you would learn to receive counsel and rebuke with all zeal. Listen now! Since you do not understand these names and you are unaware of the type of sins that draw people to them and the horror of the afflictions therein, you consider my advice as a merely human prank and not as from Jehovah God, you are unable to turn away from sin. You frown and stiffen your neck whenever you are rebuked. Take the reality that it is not an easy travail for one whose time is due even because he does not repent and remains filthy by nature. Hebrews 10:31.

4. The question then is; to where will all flesh flee? There is no refuge apart from repentance. If you hear His voice today, harden not your hearts like earlier generations. Hebrews 4:7. For this reason, anyone who teaches my words, commandments and orders for repentance should do so in all zeal and power, like a real sentry. When convincing messages are preached and the teacher demonstrates eagerness and righteousness, members will have the courage to repent, so that the blood of none is visited on a neighbour. Ezekiel 33:8-9. It will be a woeful time of great lamentation on the judgement day, to find that it was a leader's lifestyle or actions that led sheep astray on the day of reckoning; their blood will be visited on their leaders for they have made the Lord a liar. Do the scriptures not say that you are of great price? The human deserves worthy value. The promise is that not even a strand of hair will be missing, says the Lord Jesus. Luke 21:18 & 12:7. If due to human

actions the promise will be void, will such a soul find solace?

5. I, therefore, advise you who are counseling like leaders, to be alert and make fervent prayers, so that whenever you proclaim the word, you will be endowed with the truth and convincing messages that will draw souls home. In the absence of this, if wily ways are mixed with the order of God when teaching people, it will not go well with people found on the path of falsehood. Now, take this to them that whoever is captured and a slave, should strive to gain their freedom.

6. Let all of you gospel preachers, priests and teachers of the word know that I have chosen you to make your lives examples, so that when you proclaim the freedom found in righteousness those who learn this truth will be free. Being set free depends on the extent to which one can provide a favourable accounting on the day of judgement. Look! The court is already set and Jehovah God will

surely judge the nation. Hebrews 10:30. You are aware of the existence of places like Hades, the Abyss and Hell and their dreadful nature is known to you. Why then do nations not understand the present day in order to repair their hearts? Look! The judgement day of Jehovah is at hand and it is only men of righteous hearts who will be saved. There shall be no mercy for the foolish and the lazy. Revelation 11:18.

7. If your actions draw you into the midst of Hade's dwellers, strive for relief that you may become a partaker in eternal life, for there is no chance of self-defense in the Abyss; woe unto the souls that fall from grace and find themselves in this dreadful place. The power of death pushes souls to Hades. There is however a difference between the inhabitants of the Abyss and those of Hades. The Abyss is not meant for the habitation of souls, but rather for fallen angels and all varieties of demons. Powers that are separated from the arm, the might and the grace of God have their place in the Abyss.

8. Hades is the resting place of all souls and is more habitable than the Abyss. Dragon has no power over Hades because Jesus, the Lord reigns there He is the Lord of Lords and Almighty and He possesses the key to the Abyss and conquers it. Revelation 9:1.

9. Now, let me relate to you the mystery of Hades, the Abyss and the bottomless pit. Look, the souls of the dead, from the beginning of the world till today are in Hades, and they have been locked up there until the work of all shall be tested with fire. One whose get burnt shall lose it but he shall be received as one taken through fire. 1 Corinthians 3:14-15. He asked me, what does it mean when one is received through fire? And I answered, Lord, please, this is known to you alone, so kindly help me to understand your words. He exclaimed it does not displease me to unravel these mysteries to you. Pay attention therefore and be alert and listen. Demons in the Abyss continue to fight with the souls in Hades, just as they do with the living on

earth. The living fight war with prayers and so do the inhabitants of Hades. If a soul is conquered in Hades, it is drawn into the Abyss to become the Satanic agent. If one is able to fight in Hades and become an inheritor of eternal life, such a soul is considered as having been received through fire.

CHAPTER 24

FIGHTING SIN

The meaning of "dust thou art and unto dust shalt thou return" refers to those who are not able to overcome sin and are weakened by the power of death. Death leads them to Hades, where they are locked up in wait for the great day of judgement. Some humans are able to fight sin and conquer temptation and its power, according to the order laid down and so they are carried away to Paradise. This is because they have conquered the deception of sin that keeps them under the power of Hades. For this reason, death and Hades have no power over them.

2. The wages of sin is death. Presently, Jesus the Lord has given you power over death and Hades, to

the extent that all being well, you will be transfigured and go to Heaven without tasting death and Hades. Mathew 16:18. The demons of the Abyss and their commander, Apollyon are at war with humans and are deceiving them to the extent that they are unable to conquer the power of sin in order to be freed from death and Hades. The power given to you by Jesus, the Lord over death and Hades, provides you an opportunity to conquer sin with good, so the power of death will be weakened. If you are able to overcome sin, then death and Hades will have no power over you. Romans 12:21. The prophecy will then manifest that death is swallowed in victory; you death, where is your sting? You Hades, where is your strength? 1 Corinthians 15:54-55; Hosea 13:14; Isaiah 25:8.

3. Sin causes the sinner to succumb to the power of death and death renders him unto Hades. If a person's lifestyle deserves a stay in Hades but he is able to redeem himself, he is forgiven; if not he is

pushed into Abyss. The colleague of Abyss is Hell.
Look! The wages of sin is death. Romans 6:23.
Death sends souls to Hades where they are given
the chance to redeem themselves, and without
which they are pushed into the Abyss. Avoid sin,
therefore, so death will have no victory over you.

CHAPTER 25

OVERCOMING SIN MEANS OVERCOMING DEATH AND HADES

Turn unto that which is good so you will have the everlasting reward of life. Look! If you believe in God and you repent and tread perfectly on the order given you, then you will receive the power that Jesus the Lord has given His church over death. Hades and the Abyss or Hell. will then have no power over you. Mathew 16:18. Look! Your human's victory over death and Hades was revealed and it was testified that this is the mystery that, on the day of rapture, at the sound of the great trumpet, the flesh shall be changed and be clothed with immortality in a twinkle of an eye and transported to Heaven. 1 Corinthians, 15:51-52.

2. Those who will be transfigured are people whose lifestyles overcome sin and sin has no power to give them up to death. People who have been conquered by death and are locked up in Hades but have struggled to obtain redemption shall waken up from their sleep to be clothed in immortality and everlasting glory. Daniel 12:1-2.

3. The unalterable truth is that Hades will be commanded to release all who are allowed to return, whichever means of death sent them to Hades; whether by drowning in the sea or through death in caves, for the power of death and Hades shall be swallowed by then. Revelation 20:13-15. Isaiah 25:8; 1 Corinthians 15:54. Blessed and glorious are those found worthy and are given power by righteousness over the Abyss, death and Hades. Yes! They will share in the first resurrection. Look! The firm order is that Hades will release all the dead in its custody, the sea will do the same, but the Abyss will not. For this reason, therefore, take care to do right with fervent prayers and by

fighting the good fight so that Hades and the Abyss will not have any power over you.

4. Look! The goodness promised by God must be found in men for their souls to inherit everlasting life. Luke 2:13-14. It is only by the power of Jesus, the Lamb, that forgiveness can be obtained and souls are eligible for the first resurrection. Listen to what is said about the second death.

CHAPTER 26

THE SECOND DEATH AND THE LAKE OF FIRE

Satan is the one who deceives the whole world, and he is the ruler of the Abyss. Since there always exists an opportunity for human-kind, by the mercy of God, to find salvation, Satan is always trying to tempt men. If he is unable to do so during their life-time, he tries to block the soul's path. Look, he even tries to tempt angels, who are spirit. Jude 6. In much the same way, Satan tries to fight for the souls of the dead in an effort to draw them into straying.

2. Look! Hades is the resting place for the souls of the dead and there, they wait for the Almighty, until judgement day which will be pronounced on the man of sin, and he and his handiwork will be

condemned. Job 14:13. The warfare in Hades is unbearable for the flesh. Therefore, it behoves a soul which does not share in the first resurrection, to fight and overcome Hades. A soul overcoming Hades can have likened to a human being walking through a burning fire from the beginning to the end. This means that there is an opportunity in Hades for the soul to fight for liberation; it is only in the Abyss that this chance does not exist.

3. When a soul is frightened by the fire and avoids the fierceness of the pain involved, it is left beyond the fire. When the Lord Jesus entered Hades, He took many of them to eternity. 1 Peter 4:6. It is the breath of the Living God that will serve as the fire to prove the work of men as well as the inhabitants of Hades. If they persist and pass through the breath of fire exhaled by the living God, they will enter eternity. Isaiah 30:33; Mark 9:49.

If Moses had concealed some vices at the time this fire revealed itself to him, the burning bush would have consumed him. Exodus 3:2-5. It is due to the pleasure I found in Moses that the burning fire did not do him any harm. Other humans also went through fire but because of the power of my name, no harm befell them. The question then is, who are righteous enough among you to stay with Jehovah and not be consumed by the burning fire? Isaiah, 33:14-17. This scripture explains that it is only sin and the one who commits it is burned by Jehovah in the Burning Fire. Righteous people live with Him.

4. Be aware that the works of everyone shall be tested in fire and if consumed, it will be lost but the person himself will be accepted as one who has gone through fire. 1 Corinthians 3:13-15. Son of man, Listen! The meaning of this scripture is that when a human being dies, he goes to Hades and his struggle to get out, is just as fierce as passing through fire. Since all these mysteries are hidden from you humans, anytime you are counseled with my words, you do not take them seriously and do not understand that compliance is imperative for

your salvation. However, whoever rejects My words of counsel and refuses to repent, is sure to have his own blood visited on him.

5. If you find your neighbour treading the path of sin and you do not advise him to change so that his life will be saved, then that sinner will die for his sins but you will be required to account for his blood. But if you counsel him twice or thrice and he remains obstinate, then you have saved your own life and his blood will be visited on him, not you. The visitation of blood on one's head means that there is no opportunity for mercy or grace whatsoever, in this life or in the life to come. He only has to be counted among those in the Abyss to be taken for a demon. Such people are like immortals plagued with crises, suffering and affliction are their lots, forever and ever. Mathew 10:28.

CHAPTER 27

THE ABYSS AND THE DEEP PIT

Look, this is the cause of a soul being consigned to the Abyss. If it is drawn by vice into Hades and is unable to withstand it as one who is taken through fire, then Hades pushes him into the Bottomless pit and at the far end of the Bottomless pit, is the Abyss. It is the Bottomless pit that separates redeemable souls - inhabitants of Hades - from dead souls, or inhabitants of the Abyss. Luke 16:26. The dead that shall be part of the first resurrection is considered separately. There is a chasm between the inhabitants of Hades, who still have the chance if they fight hard to inherit the kingdom, and the inhabitants of the Abyss, for whom there is no hope. It is horrific. Look! I will throw away all stray spirits and souls, who have fallen into the Abyss and their portion shall be brimstone and a lake of fire, forever.

2. You who counsel people, therefore, do so in perfection and without blemish; and you who are listening to their counsel, be righteous by complying with instructions so that none of you stray be consigned to the Abyss. Apply my instructions to circumcise your hearts because the uncircumcised heart and the fallen have the same portion in the Abyss. Ezekiel 32:25. The visitation of one's blood on oneself or one's neighbour signifies that all gates of grace are shut, and the soul's direct destination is the Abyss and from there Hell is entered without further judgement. Psalms 30:9. The fallen are the stray angels frayed by God's sword and they are locked up in the Abyss. Let none of you be taken up with them because of hardheartedness for there is only everlasting humiliation. Ezekiel 32:29. Be careful therefore that

no one's blood is visited on himself or his neighbour. If renowned kings hardened their hearts and did not find it easy in Hades, do not ever think of having it easy if you refuse to repent. Ezekiel 32:31-32.

3. Disobedience leads to hard-heartedness and hard-heartedness leads to sin and the wages of sin is death. If it thus happens that if you become disobedient, then you are on the path of death. This path leads to the Abyss, where dwell those who are separated from the arms of God. This is everlasting perdition. Psalms 88:4-7.

4. Look! Obey my instructions in order to have a place of rest for your souls so you will flee from the wrath of God. Isaiah 28:22. Look!Sin has locked you human beings up in the world and you have become slaves to the power of the Abyss. The Lord Jesus, however, has brought you the opportunity for liberation. Therefore, so long as you remain alive, strive and fight to hold onto the freedom of

life and not the slavery of sin. The Dragon is making every effort to deceive you and draw you into Abyss in order to make himself king over you. Meanwhile, it is to his everlasting disgrace that he has been kicked down into the Abyss where he has been fighting to become king. Look! He who cannot be likened even to the dead is the one who makes himself king in the Abyss. Be alert and pray; so as to be steadfast in the truth in order to have eternal life, so that your place of abode is not changed by the Dragon. Isaiah 14:11-15.

5. If an angel goes astray, it is thrown into the Abyss and so does this happen to all souls who are separated from the arms and grace of Jehovah God. Be aware that Hades is not under the control of Satan. It is a place where souls are locked up awaiting the great day of the Lord; the day of judgement. Since Hades is not under Satan's control, he and his stray agents have been fighting the inhabitants of Hades just as they are fighting the living on earth. The devil even shakes the

inhabitants of Hades intending to threaten them to submit to him. Isaiah 14:9. The Abyss is the reserved abode for Satan and those who go there become worthless. Isaiah 38:17-18. The demonic agent ruling the Abyss is called Apollyon. Revelation 9:11. It is the same demon ruling the air, in the power of the present days of darkness and will is going to expose itself openly on the appointed day and, wage war against saints and the Holy Spirit, but will never win, so will he and all who he has deceived go to Hell.

6. Grace, however, provides that Hades and the oceans shall release the dead in their custody, but the Abyss will lock up its own. It is proclaimed, "Hades, where lies thy strength and death, where is thy sting?" All will be swallowed and want to hide under the power of victory. Hosea 13:14; Isaiah 25:8. These are prophecies that will, by all means, be fulfilled. Look, make sure you are not taken up together with the Abyss-bound, for anyone who goes to Abyss is separated from the arms of I,

Jehovah God and My spirit will not remember him. When finally, the Lord Jesus shall shake all Heaven and earth and even under the earth, then the ferocity of Satan will cease and the humans and Hade's dwellers will say "See he who claimed to be almighty, he is now as weak and worthless as we are. He has never been stronger than you, but he only baffled you into believing that he rules over you. Isaiah 14:10. By this, you will realize that the Abyssis far worsethan Hades.

7.Hades will release all souls in its custody for them to be tested and the work of everyone will be proved in fire. All souls able to withstand the fire shall be saved. The breath of Jehovah God will be the fire of proof. I Jehovah, the Burning Fire. Yes! I will test everyone and his works with fire. Isaiah 30:33; Deuteronomy 4:24.

Know that the Abyss and the bottomless pit will not release souls for judgement like Hades; those souls will have no opportunity for redemption. From the bottomless pit, one is pushed into the Abyss and then Hell and they will abide there forever. The order is that Satan shall be subdued under the feet of those he deceived on earth who died and then went to Hades. This is an unbearable situation for him, that is the reason for which he cunningly deceives people in order to rule over them and they submit to worshipping him, the place they lay him is on worms. Isaiah 14:19-20. It is an unalterable fact that righteous men and evil men will not share the same inheritance. All who are offspring of the devil should be aware that their evil generation and their deeds will be found together with the Abyss bound. Ezekiel 32:23-25.

8. The Lord's voice is still sounding today, and my words are His instructions so that when your earthly shed is demolished, you shall be given an everlasting shed. If you, however, reject His instructions and die in hard-heartedness then your sins will cling to your bonesand you will become worthless. Ezekiel32:27, How can bones attached

to sin be revived? You will only abide with the Abyss-bound and be like the fallen who are struck by God. Ezekiel 32:28. Son of man, let it be clear to you that you need to pray to be favoured by My words of prophecy, for the Lord God is ever ready to make manifest the prophecy for you. Deuteronomy 30:6. Jeremiah 4:4.

9. Remaining uncircumcized in the heart is a spiritual malady. Humility and obedience to instructions will have your hearts circumcised so that, you will be able to love the Lordyour God and do according to His instructions accurately. May the Lord Jesus change your hearts through the power of His blood sacrifice and take off the foreskins so you can offer a perfect sacrifice to the Living God. Hebrews 9:13-14. If you fail to ask for power through prayers, you will not be able to do the will of God in accordance with the requirements of the time. And if you commit too many sins, then your sins will lay charges against your souls, because your testimony provides that:

"Blessed are those who die in the Lord from hence. Yes, the spirit says they shall have a rest from their labours and their deeds shall follow them. Revelation 14:13. Whoever shall hold onto hardheartedness will lose his soul. One who takes pleasure in sin and loves to commit it should know that Jehovah God is a burning fire. Psalms 97:3; Hebrews 2:12-13.

10. Here is an elaboration about this fire. The fierceness of this fire supersedes any fire known to you human beings. It is a fire that burns evil things alone, for this reason, if the filth of any vice or the dirt of any evil gets near it, it consumes it instantly. If there is no dirt from sin, the fire can burn over a person without causing any harm. It burns sin only because sin is its adversary. For this reason, anybody who commits sin and takes pleasure in it should expect the fire of the wrath conserved for adversaries. Hebrews 10:26-27.

11. I told Moses not to get close because he had strangled someone to death in revenge and has not made any sacrifices for atonement. Look! Even though Moses did not hold this sin to his heart and is even likely to have forgotten it, its actions were shown on his soul. My mercy and grace bestowed on him was the order given him not to draw close, for he intended to get very close to observe the burning thicket, being God, the consuming fire which was there. Exodus 3:2-5. The fire burning without consuming the thicket is an indication that the thicket has no sin. So, will it happen that if you are holy, without sin, God Jehovah will pass over you without you being burned and that will increase your strength and sanctify you the more. My grace and mercy towards the nation was in the order given them near Mount Sinai, not to cross beyond the base so they would not touch the mountain and die. Exodus 19:21-22. God's consuming fire descended onto the mountain and it was the same Moses I instructed to climb the

mountain and come to Me and stand before My presence, for he had sacrificed for his sins.

CHAPTER 28

THE LORD'S SUPPER AND THE TREE OF LIFE

This sacrifice of atonement came to you, today's generation through the Lord Jesus, to believe in His name and turn your hearts unto His teachings. The salvation order which came through Jesus the Lord is that one should test himself well before eating of His flesh and drinking of His Covenant; the Blood Cup. 1 Corinthians 11:28-29. If anyone should harden his heart and be unworthy to drink of the cup and eat of the bread because of unrighteousness, such a one is already guilty. One who will eat and drink in worthy righteousness, however, will gain power and well-being from it, for it is the healing power of the nations.

2. The Tree of Life is already by the side of the Living River of the Holy Spirit and is bearing fruit according to the order; twelve fruit each month. Revelation 22:2. Why is it required to bear twelve fruit every month? It bears fruit thus in fulfillment of the prophecy by Ezekiel. Ezekiel 47:12. Look! The Son of Man, who was crucified, who rose from the dead on the third day is the Tree of Life. Yes! It must bear fruit every month in fulfillment of the prophecy in your present-day; that He renews your feathers so that your youthfulness is rejuvenated in the likeness of an eagle. Isaiah 40:29-31. Psalms 103:5. The purpose of the Tree of Life bearing 12 fruit every month, is for those whom the fruit is born to eat them, in accordance with the time they secure salvation.

The order accompanying the Tree of Life is that so long as you eat of this bread and drink of the cup, you are announcing the death of the Lord until He shall come back. The phrase, "so long as", does not indicate any fixed time or period. A time-line and fixed period have however, been determined, in accordance tothe performance of the order given in Heaven. It no longer only indicates the announcing of His death but is also a sign of healing, in which case eating the fruit every month at the appropriate time, provides divine healing.

3. This is what I emphasize when I tell you that believers must eat the fruit of this tree every month and must reckon that it is consumed twelve consecutive times, annually. If you excuse yourselves you have sin and by failing to eat the fruit, you deny yourselves peace and freedom. If you dodge the consumption of the fruit by making excuses or fail to take it according to the Heavenly order, then you must know that you are destroying your portion of everlasting life as provided by the Tree of Life. It is written that "Father thy will be done on earth as it is in Heaven."

4. This sacrament should be observed on earth as it is in Heaven. Therefore, if someone eats it six times

in a year, then it should be known that no Tree of Life bears fruit six times in a year. If one eats it fifty times or numerous times, it should be known that no Tree of Life bears fifty fruit or countless fruit in a year. Anyone who consumes it in this manner will likewise lose his portion of the power vested in the Tree of Life. One must eat the fruit of the Tree of Life once a month and twelve times a year, according to its fruit-bearing times.

5. If the congregation is ready but the priest fails to renew their feathers by giving them the fruit according to the Heavenly order, then the priest must be able to answer to souls who are ready but have not been given the fruit according to the Heavenly Order. Look! The proclamation that whatever you bind on earth shall also be bound in Heaven and whatever you loose on earth shall be loosenedin Heaven, does not mean that humankind has unbridled free will. If you shall bind a thing on earth, be assured it is bound according to the will of God, for this is a sign of the power that is the key

to Heaven. Therefore, if you are blind to the order and lead the people with laziness and weakness, it shall remain an iniquity against you in the presence of Heaven.

6. I, Jehovah God will raise a query on this by all means, for the weakness and excessive excuses from priests and servants of God are leading many souls astray. Look! The pronouncement of the Sentry Armour Bearer is fulfilled on them like the shepherds who drink the milk of their flocks and make for themselves protective outfits and peace-seeking garments with the wool of their flocks. Ezekiel 34:1-6. Look! They have made a covenant with laziness and weakness on earth, so they only do that which gives them ease. It should be known that if someone proves himself worthy of eating the fruit of the Tree of Life but the priest fails to lead him to it, then that priest is slated for judgement.

7. The order is that one must examine oneself before eating the fruit of the Tree of Life. Now If the priest leads the congregation to the Tree, but somebody examines himself and fails to eat it accordingly, then the priest is free from that person's query. If the people are worthy but it is because of the priest's failing that they are not able to eat the fruit of the Tree of Life according to the prescribed order, then woe betides all concerned. Look! Which priestly burden do present-day priests have, which can be likened to the burdens of the old covenant priests? The olden day priests were constantly engaged in priestly assignments throughout the whole year. If you recollect the commencement era of the New Covenant, one foundation priest testified saying: Lord, Look! We have abandoned our homes, children and plantations and have followed you. What then is our reward? He said to this foundation priest that whoever renders good service shall have a fitting

reward and likewise he who offers bad service shall receive a fitting reward.

8. Now then, son of man, take it to them that, whatever you shall bind on earth shall be also be bound in Heaven and whatever you shall unbind on earth shall be unbound in Heaven. That which you shall bind in this case is to comply with the order of life, that all souls under your care should eat of the Tree of Life every month. This is the life-giving order. Ezekiel 20:11. My spirit is not pleased with the persistent excuses of the priests. You, who shall harden your hearts concerning these issues, particularly regarding participation in the Holy Communion according to the prescribed number and those who by their persistent excuses fail to take it, should know very well that all the affliction in Hades, the Abyss, the bottomless pit and Hell are waiting for them. When you hear My voice today, harden not your hearts into doing your hearts' bidding.

9. You son of man, as I have prescribed, the fruit of the Tree of Life should be eaten every month according to the order, so why has this become a burden for you? It is surely true that the story of the cross is foolhardy to those who are perishing but is power and life for all who believe. 1 Corinthians 1:18. If someone fails to eat that which gives life and strength or someone searches for it only to eat in vain, then they are destroying their portion in the resurrection and the power of their faith will be completely weakened. It is just like fueling a machine to work up to a specific period. If the fuel is exhausted and the work is not done, the machine must be refueled for it to continue working. If for some reason no refueling is done, how can the machine be expected to work? I declare to you that, the machine cannot work unless it is refueled, and if it is not, it will cease to run and cannot function. So it is that if you do not eat the fruit of the Tree of Life, the fire of the Holy Spirit in you will go out and you will no longer shine

in your hearts and you will lose the hope of eternal life.

10. The statement "Once you eat, you proclaim the death of the Lord until his return" has caused some people to eat the fruit more than the prescribed number by the order. This is just like the behaviour of those in the wilderness, who collected manna in excess, expecting to keep it for the next day, like one who believes salt is tasty, so he uses it without measure in his meal. If it is used according to measure, the taste is good but if used in excess, the food becomes too salty and acrid for consumption. So, it is for those who eat of the Tree of Life excessively and ignore the Heavenly order, its power is completely lost by the consumers.

11. All these things have come to pass in fulfilment of what Ezekiel prophesied about the Tree of Life. Ezekiel 47:12. It was revealed to this prophet that several fruit-bearing trees line up banks of the river. The meaning of "several trees" is that from

the beginning of the world till to date, God, through the efforts of men like this prophet, has brought the word of everlasting life to humans. It is by the efforts of these prophets and teachers that God brought the promise of life. All the species of these various trees are able to bear fruit month by month. In the Heavenly order, the Lord and a priest must be found for the New Covenant and so was the Tree Chosen by God identified and the Life given unto it. This tree was identified as to bear exactly twelve fruit every month. This is the Tree of Life.

12. Though there exist several trees, life is not given to all of them. The Tree of Life represents the twelve tribes of Israel; those who possess the promise. All who believe in Jesus must certainly be registered among one of these twelve tribes, in order to fulfill the promise that "In you shall all the tribes of the earth be blessed". Genesis 12:3. Ensure therefore that your Tree Of Life bears fruit every month and that you eat of it twelve times

every year to ensure that the purpose for which
Jehovah God makes the tree will bear fruit
accordingly to demonstrate its power and blessing
over you. I am giving you a firm order, so be alert.

13. Look! Son of man, if anybody tells you that he
has a prophecy or a vision in which Satan is
tormenting unrepentant souls in Hell, know and
declare to him that this revelation is not true. Any
understanding that makes people believe that
Satan is the power which torments in Hell is totally
false. Satan has no power over Hell so how can he
have the authority to torment souls there? If it is
the real Hell, then each and every one there will
bear his own burden. Satan himself has no respite
in the Hellfire because he is also under affliction.
The fierce heat is the warring spirit of Jehovah God,
which consumes all His adversaries. Satan is the
enemy of all righteousness. Hebrews 10:26-27.

14. The reserved place for Satan is the Abyss, but
this place is so horrific that Satan himself cannot

withstand it. The Abyss is a dreadful place and Satan fled there, knowing that God is waiting for humans to repent and that as soon as the number of chosen saints is obtained, the end will come and Satan's torture will begin, which is why he is rapidly baffling people and the whole world is complicit. This has caused the end of times to be delayed. If you humans comply with righteousness as is expected of you, the end would have come long ago. Since the number of the chosen saints is not yet obtained, Heaven is still waiting. 2 Peter 3:9-10.

15. It is not for human beings that all the afflictions in the scriptures have been established butfor demons. The kingdom of Satan will be demolished, and afflictions will torment him and all his demonic agents wherever they are until Satan himself will be bound and thrown into his original abode, from where he fled onto the earth to trouble human beings. Revelation 20:1-3.

16. Take care and guard against the guileful ways of Satan and get yourselves out of vices, so that you will be filled with the Holy Spirit of our Lord Jesus Christ, to let you flee from the world. By so doing you will not be taken with those bound for the Abyss. 2 Peter 1:3-11.

I, the first and the last testifier, the burning fire in the skies, who am clothed within the cloud, speak these words to take them to the chosen ones of My Church of the Faithful Lamb say to be alert.

17. May the Peace and the spirit of the one who stands amidst the Seven Lampstands revive you now and forevermore. AMEN. Daniel 12:4-10; Revelation 10:8-11; 1 Corinthians 14:22; Ephesians 4: 10-12.

PART TWO

THE FIFTH HORN OF THE LAMB OF GOD

CHAPTER 1

ELABORATION OF PART ONE

Why does God reveal hidden things to someone even when that person is afraid? God says his thoughts and ways are hidden from man. Psalms 92:6-7. Isaiah 55:8-11.

2. By this means of appointing such people for Himself, their messages beckon people to abide by His words. This is a divine mark on the person. Isaiah 55:3-7. The Lord promised to raise men for Himself, and in the time of the new order, He started with His son, Jesus Christ. Deuteronomy 18:15-19; Acts 3:22-23. It was with Moses that God started speaking directly to men and making them hear His voice. Exodus 19:19.

3. Due to the power of demonic spirits, Christbased the message of His prophets on what has been already written, in order that the Holy Spirit will bear witness. John 15:26-27; Acts 3:24-26.

4. Divine revelations frighten men on earth, so Heaven establishes a special covenant with the receiver who is then encouraged to explain issues to the people. Luke 1:5-20. The shepherds in the field were very much terrified even though the angel which revealed himself to them brought a message of peace. Luke 2:8-10. God examines the courage of the people he appoints before revealing His messages to them.

5. Observe Ezekiel: Ezekiel 1:1-12. It is by the level of straying and the might of demonic capture that the glory of the Lord descends to strengthen the prophet not to be afraid. Ezekiel 2:1-7. The Eagle's wings. Exodus 19:3-6. In this revelation, it was observed that the Lord turned Himself into a mighty General to match the might by which

Satanic forces conquered the church, in order to deliver the people from Satan's captivity.

6. The likeness in which the Lord revealed Himself to John is almost the same as the one in which He revealed Himself to you, Victor. The manner in which the Dragon revealed itself to John is also the same in which he revealed himself to you Victor. It was frightening how he saw the Lord, and equally frightening how the Dragon appeared. Examine therefore the two frightening things and their attributes and you will get the courage to have faith in the revelation. Revelation 12:1-6.

7. The Lord adorned His full divine, military regalia in order to atone for the sins of the nation and cleanse it for obeying His words. Titus 3:3-7. It is by the strength of the weaknesses in the seven churches of Asia that the Lord's glory has been revealed to John, since he was the one to be sent. In the same vein, the weakness of your previous church, and the one established later have

weaknesses evident in the present world, which are the same as the weaknesses evident in the time of John. This is the reason that you, Victor should see the Lord in His full military apparel. Revelation 1:12-16.

8. It is by the sight of this divine image that the church has become one with the Faithful Lamb. This image must be remembered at all your Lord's Supper rituals and the practice should be maintained throughout all generations. Exodus 12:11-14. Before the nation ate the Passover Lamb, their preparedness indicated they were warriors on a mission. A nation to be delivered today should also prepare itself in like manner for war, to defend their Lord, the Savior. The church of today should learn about spiritual preparedness by following the rules of the Holy Spirit in the New Testament era, just as the people of the Old Testament prepared themselves for Jehovah God to deliver them out of captivity. Ephesians 6:10-20.

9. When Ezekiel saw the Lord's glory, it was later revealed to him how the nation got destroyed and needed rehabilitation. When the Lord revealed Himself to John on the isle of Patmos, he revealed the weaknesses of the seven churches to him so they would repent. So did the Lord reveal all the destruction going on in the church through demonic forces, to you. One was like the viper which is the venomous old serpent that since the time of the Garden of Eden, has destroyed the peace and freedom of men. It was revealed to John the Baptist during his time, how the viper had by cunning ways claimed men for itself. Mathew 3:7-8. Does the Lord not have the right to rise and save this generation of men from the viper? The Lord Jesus in his time, also saw how humans had become offspring of the viper and the need to deliver them from its grip. Mathew 23:33-34; 1 John 3:8-9.

10. Anytime God intends to reveal something, Satanattempts to first reveal a false version to

deceive people. But when the real revelation of the Lord comes and the prophet is not confused, the Lord continues to make clear all His prophecies. You Victor, your revelation started with the vision of a toad. Thereafter, the Lord revealed Himself in a war-like and war prepared manner. This is the image He gave as a fortress for the prophet, so that no matter the powers of false revelations, the prophet would never be deceived.

11. Use the revelation of Ezekiel to explain these things. Ezekiel 1:1-28. Most prophecies begin just as a person goes to meet his enemies in war. It is to be noted that before Heaven sends a revelation to earthly men to receive and act on, there has been a prior defeat and subjugation of the demonic powers in high places that may attempt to prevent the revelation. Remember that in the days of Daniel, his revelation was blocked for twenty-one days. Daniel 10:1-19. Because of the presence of a multitude of Demonic forces, it is not easy to send

a revelation to earth. Heaven, therefore descends in full military warfare.

12. When the Lord traded arguments with the devil in order to save his people, He revealed himself to Ezekiel, in a manner like the enemies' preparedness. He revealed a cloud of thick smoke to Ezekiel. Ezekiel 1:4. This vision meant that Jehovah was in search of the enemy to destroy them all. Psalms 97:1-7. When the Lord faces his enemies and the need arises to use fire, Jehovah does not hesitate. He therefore always moves with these weapons.

13. In his vision, Ezekiel saw an image that resembled a human being. Ezekiel1:5-9. If the Lord is moving and there is a need to encounter a human being in that situation, he turns His human face to the person so that no harm is caused to the seer. Ezekiel studied all these things about Jehovah God. Ezekiel 1:10-11. The face of a human being stands for the salvation of men. Leviticus 4:13-21;

Judges 6:19-24. In this case, no harm befell Gideon because He showed him grace and turned His human Face to him. Ezekiel's vision of the face of a lion was indicative of the Lord's mighty arms of war if there was fierce warfare. 2 Kings 17:24-28. In this case, also, the Lord turned the lion's face towards the nation until it was time to raise the priest who would turn the hearts of the people into fear of the Lord.

14. The prophet who could not abide by the rules of the Lord, but did what displeased him was met by the Lord, who turned His face of a lion to him. A lion came to devour that young prophet. A man who happens to observe the will of the Lord and receives the image of a lion from the Lord is able to defeat his enemies all the time. Genesis 49:8-10.

15. You are exhorted in the same manner to endeavour to do good so that the blessing of the Lord may be fulfilled for you. When Ezekiel saw the face of an angel, it stood for the Lord's deliverance

from the hands of the enemy. Exodus 19:3-6; Revelation 12:13-14. Pray therefore to be endowed with the blessings of the eagle. Isaiah 40:28-31.

16. All prophecies are revealed to show the level to which the church or the nation has fallen and strayed. Since the Lord Jesus has revealed Himself to you, you Victor will no longer be frightened or harmed by any further revelations. In the case of John, Jesus prepared and revealed Himself to show the level and manner of the weaknesses of the seven churches. The image by which Jesus reveals himself has the power of overcoming weakness. An example is that you Victor, saw Jesus first, before visions of the devil appeared. This is indicative of the fact that Jesus has conquered all the enemies. The first vision reveals that which consumes the faith of men to exhaustion. – a cat and a mouse – Luke 18:7-8; Luke 17:5-6. The second vision which shows the serpent spitting on the church indicates the aim of the serpent to lay claim on the members of the church.Mathew 12:33-35

17. The machinations of the toad, which is the third vision, abounds in the church. Revelation 16:12-14. Thunderstorms are also indicative of God's might. Psalms 29: Be careful therefore about lip service when worshipping. Mark 7:5-7. Remember that it is the works of Abomination of Desolation that will lead even the selected few to fall. Mathew 24:24-25. Righteous people will get assistance from Heaven to stand firm. Proverbs24:15-16.

18. The vision of the second revelation is that the Beastthat came out of the sea to fight a war. Revelation 13:1-10. Jesus revealed Himself to John on the Island of Patmos and His image looked almost like the revelation you had of Him. Understand this to mean that it is almost the same weaknesses found in the seven churches that are evident in the churches of today. His pure white hair is an indication of His unchanging nature forever and ever. He changes his eyes into fighting eyes. Psalms 11:4-5. If he examines someone with

his eyelashes and observes unrighteousness in the person, he fixes his gaze on the enemy to make him fall. Psalms34:12-17. God expects men to be unblemished in all things when He stretches his eyes to examine them. Job 31:29-35.

19. If God or Jesus stretches His right hand to someone, it means whatever God wants to do through that person shall surely come to pass and nothing can prevent its manifestation. Proverbs 16:1-5. It is the Lord's spirit that shows those who deserve to be on the right hand of God. Hebrews 8:1-2; Psalms 110:1; 1 Corinthians15:25; Hebrews 10:12-15; Ephesians 1:15-23. When he turns his feet like red hot brass, they are used to crush the heads of His enemies. He shall smite nations with the sharp double-edged sword that comes out of His mouth. Revelation 19:11-16.

20. The Lord in his revelation indicated how He shared Himself with the various churches. The needs of the first church are indicated in Revelation

2:1-3, for them to be complete so that, the Lordwould give them the power of His full salvation. The Lord also made available another image to the second church. Revelation 2:8-11. This church was found to be steadfast in the teachings of the beginning and the end; they were left only with how to hold to these faithfully till the end.

21. That of the third church is found in Revelation 2:12-15. The first church hated the doctrine of Nicolaitans which the Lord also hates, but this third church approved of the doctrine of Nicolaitans and many others. Do you not have such examples in The Church of the Faithful Lamb? In the case of the church which follows, they were found to have received doctrines that would not permit the Lord's image to be shared by them to do its work of salvation. Revelation 2:18-20. The Lord shall punish churches that insist on using other doctrines.Ephesians 4-14-20

22. In the case of the church which followed this one, He promised them His seven spirits. Revelation 3:1-3. By strengthening this church, they are required to hold fast to this doctrine so that its power will save them. Revelation 3:7-11. The other churches abide by carnal desires and cannot account for their lack of spiritual standing. Revelation 3:14-20. In the case of Ezekiel's revelation, even though the visions were frightening, he was able to stay among them easily.

23. The chariot wheels move together with the Cherubim because the spirit of the Cherubim is in them. Ezekiel stood among them peacefully because the spirit of the Cherubim entered him. These are the things to be done by the church for the spirit of the Cherubim to descend into them. The eyes of the Cherubim represent the power of God's mercy. Ezekiel 9:1-11. The eyes of the Cherubim are so numerous that nothing can be hidden from them. Ezekiel 10:9-15. They are called "Whirlwinds" because it is on the wings of the wind

that they move. It is to be noted that before anything occurs on earth, it is planned among the Cherubim, whether fortune or misfortune. Ecclesiastes7:13-14.

24. People are damned if they do not receive the sign of the Lord's grace. But people who stay awake in prayer are critically marked by the eyes of the Cherubim. 2 Corinthians 6:1-5; Luke 18:7-8. The Lord exhorts you to "Be watchful and pray so that you do not fall into temptation". The church seriously needs to have night prayers for the sake of the Cherubim, so that their all-seeing eyes will have mercy on you.

25. For one who abides faithfully by the laws and is strengthened by the growth of the laws in him, the Cherubim reflect the image of God in the likeness of a lion to that person so such people resemble a lion in spirit. Genesis49:8-12. If we obey Him and do His will, He shall change us into His likeness. And so between the church and the Cherubim, you shall

appear like a lion among lions and demonic lions shall be destroyed. 1 Peter 5:7-9.

26. A church that undertakes fasting and prayers seriously and follows the laws shall have the Cherubim easily descend on its members. It is important that the church knows the faces of the images revealed by the Cherubim. The face of the bull stands for the church that has been given the power and realization to engage in the worship of atonement in the presence of the Lord. Leviticus 23:26 – 32; 2 Corinthians 5:18 -19

27. Atonement is very important and makes the Cherubim vigilant to ensure that no harm will bypass the power of the atonement to strike the church. It is the spirit of the Cherubim that divinely opens the eyes of priests to institute the doctrine of atonement in their churches. 2 Corinthians 5:20-21. Jehovah God knows the nation will, by all means commit some sins, so He taught Moses what

rituals to perform to make atonement.
Leviticus16:29-34; Leviticus 8:14-17.

28. There are several versions of fasting and prayers but the one particularly marked by the Cherubim is the one which goes together with the flesh of Jesus being received for atonement, for it is Jesus who in faith has atoned for our sins. Hebrews13:11-14. The fasting and prayers which accompany the holy meal have become the atonement worship. Colossians1:19-23. It is imperative for man to atone before God. The Cherubim take great pleasure in such church rituals. The Cherubim recognized Ezekiel because these things were up to date in him.

29. The Lord's commandment to Moses about conventions brings about the powers in the image of the Cherubim's face as that of the eagle. Leviticus 23:40-44. The wings of the Lord's eagles and the wings of the Cherubim usually stretch over the church when the whole congregation is on their

knees in prayer during conventions. This is a great sign of oneness through which the Lord blesses the church. Psalms 68:8-22. When people have a clean conscience towards each other in conventions, their prayers vibrate all parts of the Cherubim and pulldown God's power into the midst of the church for their steadfastness. It is these prayers that become thunderstorms. Psalm 29

CHAPTER 2

KEEP CONVENTION CAMPS CLEAN

Deuteronomy 23:13-15

Convention camps must be kept clean to avoid the sight of human waste or the throw outs of both children and adults. The faith must be displayed by all, to pray to uproot the roots of sin from among all, for Christ to rule in you.Colossians 3:1-8

2. Most of the visions in the revelations, are the various work of demons. It, therefore, behooves the priest and church leaders to lead and wage a war against the signs of the cats and the mice. 1 Samuel 6:10-18. Now, concerning Elymas or Barr Jessus, no one is permitted to do their will. Acts 13:4-12. Paul did not allow the female sorcerer to

go scot-free. Acts 16:16-21. Ensure that all church leaders wage war against the serpents. Isaiah 27:1-6. Jesus himself promised to send prophets to work against the serpents. Mathew 23:33-36. Though scribes could use their pens to alter things, Jeremiah 8:8-10 both fortune and misfortune come from the Lord. Ecclesiastes 7:14. Judgement comes when prescribed by God. Isaiah 29:21-24.

3. I said, "You shall see me, but the world cannot see me". John 14:22-24. It pleases Heaven that you hear my voice again because the commandments and precepts you, Victor has received from Me and have written down, demand that encouragement and elaboration be sent to you from Heaven, where these teachings come from. All the messages you previously wrote down also came through the grace of the Lord for you to write for remembrance. Isaiah 30:8-10. It is for the avoidance of arguments and doubts about the messages at your various places of worship, (where you worship truthfully) that the Lord of Host has

encouraged you Victor to write these messages and you have faithfully done so. Malachi 3:16.

4. Now, for you to teach these messages so that the church is not deceived, you have been found wanting. Therefore, I, the Morning Star of the living God, have come back to explain the remaining issues faced by the churches. I am the One holding the Seven Spirits and the Seven Stars of God and I am making these pronouncements. The self-complacent and the proud will not hear My messages. The meek and the thoughtful, however, will hear these messages and of wisdom shall be blessed by the words that proceed from My mouth, as has been written. Zephaniah 3:9-13.

5. There are people among you who speak proudly and blaspheme the Lord's prophet who is in your midst. They meet and pick quarrels against the man of God, even to the extent of laughing behind the prophet that hunger has struck his household; and that they would see how he will get out of it.

6. Understand that the vigilant eyes of the Lord are watching all men and probing their hearts. Psalms 33:12-15. There are some among you who stand against God's chosen vessel and claim that his prophecies are the reason for the hunger of his family, so he makes false pronouncements in the name of God. "He preaches due to the burden of his hunger so who can obey his words?" Blasphemy and equating oneself with the chosen vessel of God, should be known to have been recorded by the ears of Jehovah God.

7. Do you not see any sign on the man which proves to you that he has been chosen by God? Change your hearts and minds therefore to avoid the visitation of God's anger. Zephaniah 1:4-6. The word of caution therefore is that if you reject the chosen vessel of God, it is God's word you reject and not that of man. God is seeking the meek of the earth to hear these messages and turn to the words of wisdom and be blessed. Zephaniah 2:3

8. Whether people obey your messages or not, Jehovah God will not change His mind. The wrath of the Lord shall be visited on the hardhearted.

CHAPTER 3

THE ALTAR OF WITNESS

The remainder of the teachings concerns the altars of the Lord. There is a need for you to know about all the altars of the Lord and their services. There are several altars, but I will elaborate on the functions of two only because it is on these two that the functions for the salvation of humans are performed. God has chosen two altars to serve as the atonement bearers. The Lamb of God is the High Priest on the only altar on earth, for he has not been slain without an altar. Revelation 5:1-6.

2. The scriptures have pointed out the powers that constitute the God Head which is on the altar of the son of God. The altar of the Lamb of God is a "blood altar" and no meat sacrifices are made on it.

Hebrews 13:10-14; Leviticus 16:27-30. It should be clearly understood that, if blood sacrifices are made at the outskirts of the city, (by burning the sacrificial lamb whole), the priests do not remain forever at the outskirts. After completing the sacrifices at the outskirts, they have to return home. The priest, after offering sacrifices on the altar on which no meat is served will, by all means have to be served a meal; the priest also has to eat. Without this grace, no living being can serve on the altar of the Lord Jesus Christ.

3.Satan has confused people on issues concerning this Altar, to the extent that if people do not ask for an understanding of this through prayer, they will be baffled and accept odd doctrines and so perish. Hebrews 13:9. It is all blood sacrifice and the sacrifice of animals that constitute the service rules of the atonement Altar. Therefore, if the servers have no right to share of its sacrifice, how will they survive and live to continue working on it? These are the precepts of the altar on earth and they can never be changed. This is the rule about the altar of Jesus Christ.

4. The rules of the altar of Heaven are very different and offer everlasting life to those who work on it. This altar offers meals to its servers except that salaries are not established for those who serve on it. The priest who serves on the altar of Heaven is called Melchizedek, also known as the Prince of Peace in Heaven. During a congregational session on the Mount of Congregations, it was decreed that the atonement Altar of Jesus should be merged with that of Melchizedek of Heaven in the divine order of the High Priest. According to this order, therefore after the priest has completed his sacrifice and returned home, he has the right to eat, according to the Priestly order of Melchizedek. Hebrews 5:4-6.

5. It is expected of the altar that its servers learn and practice the order once the name of Melchizedek has been connected to the altar. What

then is the nature of the altar of Melchizedek? By the order of the Priesthood, it is expected that wherever He is, that place must have peace in abundance since He is the Prince of Peace. Hebrews 7:3-7. There is also the need for prayers for Heavenly intervention to understand these things. When Melchizedek descended to meet Abraham, he never came empty-handed but rather brought him bread and wine. Genesis 14:18-20. After Abraham conquered his enemies by relying on God, Melchizedek came and blessed him for defeating his enemies. Psalms 110:1-7. What you need to guard against seriously, is confounding the rules of the Altar of Jesus Christ. It is required of you by implication that you comply with all the commandments and rules of these two altars, to the letter. Then the Altar in Heaven and the Altar on earth will perform their respective assignments effectively.

6. The altar on earth has on its own provided prescriptions of what should be done on it.

Mathew. 10:7-10. The order of the Altar of Heaven is also thus prescribed: "Cater to the needs of saints and receive strangers". This implies that care must be taken for the needs of saints, whose situation may be unbearable without the intervention of the church. It is to be observed that all saints have needs of some sort and by all means, critical needs must be noted and immediately catered to.

7. The Priesthood established only according to the order of the altar of Christ cannot withstand the hardships of modern-day crises. On the other hand, the church is exposed to danger if the priesthood is established on the order of the altar of Moses and Aaron. 1 Corinthians, 9:13-14. Due to the foregoing, some churches have instituted salaries for their priests – which has also degenerated into a different problem – greed and jealousy in the holy place, one against the other. One who receives a high salary considers himself higher in rank due to monetary honour, though he may not be so

appointed. When human considerations take precedence over the will of God on the Altar, the spirit of the Lord decides not to dwell among them. God is the righteous Judge, and it is for Him to raise people or humble them. Psalms 75:5-8.

8. It is decreed that missions of grace should not be rewarded with pay. 1 Corinthians, 9:16-18. Be watchful about this scripture so you don't get trapped in the reward snares of Gehazi. When the yoke of reward befalls an Altar, it loses recognition in the face of Christ and does not also belong to Melchizedek. It changes to an Altar of feeding and a search for a reward which changes churches with such Altars into money-making business churches.

9. It is absolutely imperative to understand and to establish that no monetary reward be attached at all, so as not to flout the rules of the Altar. Rather, the labour of the scriptures should be strengthened with mercy and grace in order to avoid the temptations of greed and jealousy which have the

tendency of driving you apart. The priest must willingly inform the church leadership of his important needs – which the leadership ought to understand and decide whether to lend support or not so that in case of a fault, its source can easily be identified in Heaven.

10. So, too should the elders of the church be equally watchful and observant to see to it that the Lord in Heaven is using the prophet in all ways, even in his sleep. The Lord is using all his belongings, so the elders should be observant to ensure that he does not undergo serious crises that may lead the church into the hands of Satan. The unsteadfastness of the pastor opens the floodgates of weakness for Satan. 1 Timothy 3:1-7. Satan takes pleasure in using all the scriptures when making charges against righteous people, but the devil will be scared away provided you are vigilant. But you Victor, have a different case. The matter in which the devil always wishes to trap you is how a man should properly care for his household. The devil

has observed your inability to be steadfast in this and is therefore making efforts to defeat you.

11. Most of the time, Heaven does not accept the charges made against you, because it is observed in Heaven that the Lord is using all your belongings for doing His work. Sometimes, circumstances compel people you pray for to be saved from their temptations to move and join your household. If the housekeeper is not able to cater adequately for such people, then Satan uses it as a charge against you. But if it is observed from Heaven that the fault is not yours Victor, then the scriptures say that "God intervenes at sunrise" Look, there are a lot of people among you whose households do not receive even one single stranger for a whole year. Some are not even able to entertain their own relations or provide them any support.

12. Many of them think and regard you Victor, in the same manner. Look, Satan makes charges against the church and most of the time intends to

lay these charges on you, Victor. But if it is observed from Heaven that the fault is not yours Victor, then "God intervenes at sunrise". The church should be well aware that the one it pleases God to use is you, Victor and the household that should be used to save people for God is Victor's household.

13. There are some people among you who have warned others not to enter you, Victor's house to avoid insult. Look! I am the fifth-morning star among the horns of Jesus, the Lamb of God. I have spoken these words in the hearing of the church. All those who think that you Victor, will be disgraced in all these cases are disappointed – they should change their mind and see if they can be saved. Now, those of you who come to meet people in Victor's house and blaspheme them, whereas you yourselves do not have the grace, should be warned to desist from this unwholesome behaviour. If anybody meets some visitors in Victor's house, they should rather pray that the

Lord should shower his grace on Victor so you are able to feed the people and reserve residues, so that God will heal them in time for them to go home in peace.

All these guiding instructions have been sent down to you for your correction and repentance so that a straight path can be designed for generations yet unborn. Therefore, do not harden your hearts in these cases. The messages of I, the fifth horn of Jesus Christ, has come to an end.

14. Counsel yourselves with these divine instructions. Hosea 8:11-14. You are not the genesis of the wishes of God. Nehemiah 12:44-47. These precepts exist solely for the nations of God. 2 Chronicles 19:8-11. The people of Israel move in groups with their leaders. Numbers 10:21-28. You will become a corrupt church if you do not change. 2 Chronicles 12:9-13. Pray for the guidance of Jacob. Hosea 12:13-15.